FRENCH HISTORY
AND SOCIETY
THE WARS OF RELIGION
TO THE FIFTH REPUBLIC

FRENCH HISTORY AND SOCIETY

THE WARS OF RELIGION
TO THE FIFTH REPUBLIC

Roger Mettam
and
Douglas Johnson

Revised and reprinted
from
France: A Companion to French Studies
EDITED BY D. G. CHARLTON

METHUEN

FRANCE: A COMPANION TO FRENCH STUDIES
First published in 1972
by Methuen & Co Ltd
11 New Fetter Lane, London EC4
Printed in Great Britain
by Richard Clay (The Chaucer Press), Ltd
Bungay, Suffolk
These chapters revised and first published as a
University Paperback in 1974
This edition © 1974 Methuen & Co Ltd

ISBN 0 416 81620 7

Distributed in the USA by
HARPER & ROW PUBLISHERS INC
BARNES & NOBLE IMPORT DIVISION

CONTENTS

EDITOR'S PREFACE

The chapters in this volume first appeared in *France: A Companion to French Studies* in 1972 (London, Methuen, x + 613 pp.). That work – ranging over French history and society, thought, literature, painting, sculpture and architecture, music, and politics and institutions from the Renaissance to the present – is inevitably lengthy and proportionately costly. It has thus been suggested that particular chapters which together provide a very useful treatment of their subject should be made available in cheaper format. That is the aim of the series to which this book belongs, covering respectively:

1 *French History and Society: The Wars of Religion to the Fifth Republic* (Dr Roger Mettam and Professor Douglas Johnson)
2 *French Thought since 1600* (Dr D. C. Potts and Professor D. G. Charlton)
3 *French Literature from 1600 to the Present* (Professor W. D. Howarth, Professor Henri M. Peyre and Professor John Cruickshank)
4 *French Art and Music since 1500* (Professor Sir Anthony Blunt and the late Mr Edward Lockspeiser) (with illustrations not included in the original volume)
5 *Contemporary France: Politics, Society and Institutions* (Professor Jean Blondel, in an expanded treatment of his subject)

Each study has been revised, with additional material where necessary, and the original brief bibliographies have been expanded into the form of bibliographical essays. Given 'the chastening insight [in Professor Sir Ernst Gombrich's words] that no culture can be mapped out in its entirety, but no element of this culture can be understood in isolation', one may regret that these chapters should be torn from their original context, and it is greatly to be hoped that those interested in individual elements of French culture will refer to the total volume to complete their understanding. Yet it is the Editor's belief, even so, that this present book provides, at a price which most would-be purchasers can afford, a widely informative, up-to-date guide and evaluation.

D. G. CHARLTON

Department of French Studies
University of Warwick
February 1974

FRENCH HISTORY AND SOCIETY FROM THE WARS OF RELIGION TO THE REVOLUTION

Roger Mettam

The thirty years before the accession of Henri IV to the French throne in 1589 were torn by social and religious conflict, erupting from time to time into bitter spells of civil war – the 'wars of religion' as they have been styled. During the preceding half of the sixteenth century much of Europe had been involved in the Italian wars, a series of international confrontations which had inspired Frenchmen to forget their internal differences and unite behind their two strong kings, François I and Henri II. When the wars were ended by the Peace of Câteau-Cambrésis in 1559, the same year in which Henri II met his untimely and accidental death, the country was deprived of a national purpose and dissident elements came to the fore. All the constituents of civil war were present in the succeeding years: a dissenting religious minority, whose influence had grown unchecked during the Italian wars but whose very existence was abhorrent to a Catholic monarch bearing the title of 'Most Christian King'; a series of weak or child rulers, and at times the regency of a woman and a foreigner – the Queen-Mother Catherine de Medici; powerful aristocratic factions and privileged social groups who were eager to gain authority by supporting the feeble crown against other opponents.

These 'wars of religion' were thus only partly concerned with conflicting faiths, although the combatants were always quick to emphasize the divine mission which justified their political actions. Parties formed and reformed, individuals changed sides with frequency, but a pattern can nevertheless be imposed on their battles because the core of each faction remained fairly constant. On the one hand was the ultra-Catholic party of the Guise family, who were ever amenable to the demands of the Spanish and who constituted themselves into the

Catholic League. At the other extreme were the Protestants and their supporters, ultimately led by Henri of Navarre, the most obvious candidate for the crown when Henri III should die. In the centre was the steadily increasing *politique* party, preferring peace and religious toleration to civil war and the persecution of heretics.

Whether the next king were to be a Navarre or a Guise, his first priority would have to be the establishment of a secure throne, dependent on none of these sectional interests. Yet it was not easy to devise national policies and create a single centralized government which all Frenchmen would willingly accept. France was too fragmented a collection of provinces to have any common aspirations, save against an external enemy. In certain areas, where the representative provincial Estates still met or where great and independent aristocrats held the post of governor, the royal administration seemed scarcely to acknowledge some of the directives issued by its sovereign. Only a laborious process of attrition would erode the various forms of opposition which existed throughout the kingdom and would free the crown from restraint. In the two hundred years between the accession of Henri IV and the outbreak of the Revolution, that process continued unceasingly and never achieved its target.

The history of seventeenth- and eighteenth-century France is dominated by this conflict between centralized royal government and local privilege. The crown tried steadily to extend its control over all aspects of life within the kingdom, while social groups and administrative institutions sought to preserve their varying degrees of independence and their traditional rights. The authority of the monarch was accepted unquestioningly, as long as it was confined to those matters which were generally regarded as its legitimate concern. When the royal ministers attempted to encroach upon provincial power, or stealthily to undermine the privileges of individuals, resistance was strong and widespread.

If the sphere of royal influence was thus limited, within it the absolutism of the Bourbons was unchallenged. No one suggested any means of restricting or replacing the executive power of the crown, partly because there were no individuals or institutions in the State who were fitted for the role. Those who had the ability would not have had the necessary popular support. Theorists reminded the king that France had an ancient constitution and a code of fundamental laws which he was morally bound to observe, but this was not an effective way of restraining the monarch. Nor could a petition against a particular edict be relied upon to move the hard hearts of the Paris ministers. The only way of opposing the many unpopular policies evolved by the central government was simply for the royal agents in the provinces to refuse to implement them. Throughout the years of the *ancien régime* the French crown, unlimited in its power of decision, never managed to impose its will wholeheartedly on its officials or on the country.

French Society in the Seventeenth Century

If the privileged groups in French society regarded the central government with suspicion, they showed little more affection for each other. Such social antagonisms resulted from the ill-defined nature of their rights and duties, which led to frequent disputes. Yet, whatever the tensions between them, these various smaller units – the parish, the town, the guild, the sovereign court, the province – seemed to the ordinary subject to be more easily comprehensible and relevant to his needs than the State, whose policies brought him so little benefit and so much hardship.

The First Estate of the realm, the clergy, was more frequently among the supporters of the crown than were the other two Estates. Although the higher churchmen were usually drawn from noble families, they received their benefices from the king, and were normally appointed because they had a reputation for loyalty and intelligence. Continued support of the crown was essential for further promotion within the hierarchy. The humble *curés* of the parishes were men of very different background, who had more in common with their parishioners than with their clerical superiors, but all played a crucial role in moulding the society of this highly religious age. The Church possessed fiscal privileges, of course, but it was more willing to pay its traditional 'free gift' to the crown than were the provincial Estates. The ruler, God's representative in the kingdom by Divine Right, exploited the wealth of the Church from time to time, and protests from an allegedly hard-pressed clergy resulted; but the monarch was also their only hope of defence against the attacks of the *parlements*, who consistently sought to abolish the few remaining powers of the ecclesiastical courts and were ever watchful lest Rome interfere in the affairs of France through the agency of the Church.

The nobility were even less amenable to the extension of royal power and proved a more effective obstacle. The term *noblesse* referred to a wide range of people, united only by their privileges, especially their exemption from direct taxation. Nobility was either inherited or acquired – by royal favour, by outstanding military achievements or by long or distinguished service in the bureaucracy. Because of the social prestige associated with it, especially when re-inforced by landed wealth, the men of the rich middle classes preferred to spend their profits on buying an office which sooner or later gave them noble status than to invest them in further commercial enterprises. They were then compelled to abandon all their former economic pur-suits in favour of the profits of office and the estates which they now purchased, because trade and business were forbidden to the noble by law, and the men who practised them were heartily despised by the aristocratic élite. It was a perpetual problem for royal ministers that their cherished economic schemes lacked the support of the wealthiest men in the kingdom. Even though the laws forbidding nobles to trade were modified, most of them still disdained to enter this profession which the ancestors of some noble houses had followed successfully in the not too distant past.

The influence of the nobility was everywhere in French society. In the localities they had power over the peasantry, over municipal officials and even over royal agents. In the *pays d'états*, those provinces where the representative Estates still met, they had an opportunity in these assemblies to voice the views of their order. The higher aristo-crats took a lead in provincial affairs, and might have the ear of the king or his ministers at court as well. Although many had fallen from favour in consequence of their role in the civil wars of the sixteenth century, and others would do so after the Frondes of Louis XIV's minority, there were always some nobles at court whom the kings trusted and asked for advice, despite the rise of new kinds of counsellor, and always a few who, as provincial governors, were still important and powerful royal agents in difficult provinces. The nobility were essential to the State because they provided the officers of the army and, if a few men rose from the ranks by merit alone, continued to do so during the reign of Louis XIV. Indeed that monarch, more than his two predecessors, reduced the percentage of humbler families who entered the nobility, believing firmly in maintaining the purity of his social élite.

Nobility was thus the goal in seventeenth-century France. It was discussed endlessly in the *salons* and formed the subject of the most famous plays. It was generally believed that nobles were superior beings and it therefore followed that, while they were treated with unusual respect and fairness in the courts of law, they were, if convicted, considered more guilty and were more severely punished than commoners who committed the same crimes. The aristocrat was allowed to wear finery which was forbidden to others, and his privileges were upheld by the king, even though royal agents in the localities might be attempting to undermine them surreptitiously.

The greatest nobles of all, the princes of the blood royal, were a particularly serious threat to the crown, even though their position in society was so unique that they had very little in common with other social groups, including other nobles. If they came to the fore at moments of crisis, their selfishness and arrogance rapidly disillusioned their supporters. After their behaviour in the civil wars and in the Frondes, together with their constant plotting against ministers and during minorities, Louis XIV determined to keep them under surveillance at court, showered with prestigious court offices, but detached from the spheres where their patronage was most effective. He strongly preferred the company of aristocrats to that of the new financial and trading classes on whom his revenues and the prosperity of his State depended, and was able to surround himself with large numbers of them once the court moved to its permanent home at Versailles in 1682. Yet, although a man's rank within the nobility usually determined the level of ceremonial office which the king granted to him, it bore no relation to his influence in political affairs. The favoured advisers of the king might include men of varied social backgrounds, but no kind of pedigree gave one any certainty of entering their exclusive circle. Royal favour could not be predicted. Many nobles chose instead to remain in the provinces where their influence was assured.

A distinction is often made between the *noblesse d'épée* and the *noblesse de robe*, but this is somewhat misleading. Many members of the *épée* – nobles by birth or of distinguished, if recent, military origins – did indeed despise the professional bureaucrats of the *robe*, and lived by the traditional landed wealth and military talents of their class. Others, whose financial situation was more precarious, resented that they could not afford to compete with middle-class men in purchasing these posts in the bureaucracy for themselves. A third group did buy offices or marry into leading *robe* families, and it is here that the boundary between the two kinds of nobility becomes blurred. *Robe* and *épée* might describe a man's profession, but conveyed less clear evidence about his family background.

The *noblesse de robe*, whatever their origins, formed the greatest threat to the extension of royal absolutism, even though they, as royal officials, were also its agents. The upper levels of this bureaucracy were men of immense social prestige, who wielded great power either in the sovereign courts in Paris or in the *parlements* and administrative departments of the provinces, and who married into other influential families in their institution or locality. Of all the bureaucracies evolved by the 'Renaissance states', this was the largest, and in France there was no 'country' party to challenge its power, not only because there were no effective national representative assemblies through which to do so, but because the bureaucrats tended to side with groups in the localities in opposing the policies of the royal ministers in the central government.[1]

In the early seventeenth century there was no alternative to an administrative system of this kind, which had developed fast under the later Valois and was as efficient as any of those kings might have expected. Officials passed on their posts to a relative, probably a son, who, although he had received no more specialized training than his predecessor, had at least been associated with the office before he took charge of it. Secondly there were the financial benefits which this system brought to the royal treasury, and which hard-pressed governments exploited at the cost of efficiency. If the purchase of office and subsequent ennoblement were the ambitious aims of the wealthy merchants, so too they provided the crown with a way of taxing men who were exempt from many other taxes. A proportion of the original purchase price went to the crown, after which the office-holder paid annual dues for the right to bequeath it to his descendants, and was often forced to lend money to the king at uneconomic rates. The officials largely paid themselves out of the revenues and fees they handled, which encouraged them to work harder and saved the crown a salary bill, although the central government's inadequate sources of information could not discover how often an illegal share of these profits was retained by the official. Corruption became more tempting when the ministers, seeking urgent funds, created more and more

[1] A comparison of the role played by the bureaucracy in various 'Renaissance states', as he calls them, and in the revolts of mid-seventeenth-century Europe was made by Professor H. Trevor-Roper in *Past and Present*, 16 (1959). This stimulating attempt to propound a theory of a general crisis, together with criticisms of his analysis, may be most conveniently found in Trevor Aston (ed.), *Crisis in Europe 1560–1660: Essays from 'Past and Present'* (London, 1965).

offices, all of which found eager buyers, but which antagonized existing office-holders who saw their work and its rewards divided up and shared with others. Yet, although prices of offices rose, the legal and illegal perquisities and the social prestige more than compensated for the initial outlay.

Below the privileged strata of clergy and nobility were many other stratified levels. At the top were the bourgeois, the chief citizens of the towns, exempt from direct taxation but having certain duties as well as privileges. The bourgeois of Paris were especially favoured and could be tried only by the courts of their own city. There was frequently tension between these more exalted men and the humbler townsmen who lived alongside them, made worse by the closed corporations of craftsmen and merchants which gave the leading citizens complete and selfish control over the economic life of their town or city. The townsmen paid certain dues to the municipality which was responsible for much of its own local administration, while in the countryside the peasant might pay seigneurial dues to the local lord in addition to the heavy burden of taxation imposed on him by the crown. The peasantry suffered badly during much of the seventeenth century, some being forced to abandon their land and join the bands of vagabonds who roamed the countryside or made the streets of the towns unsafe. Survival was a precarious business. If the average woman had twelve children, six would die within a year, while plague, starvation through bad harvests and other hazards would reduce still further the number who reached maturity. Forty was an unusual age to achieve. The distance from normal existence to starvation was so short that one bad crop could bring disaster to an entire province.

Direct taxation thus weighed heavily on these lower and poorer levels of society, because so many other groups were exempt from it. A perennial problem for the royal ministers was how to tap the wealth of the privileged for the benefit of the State, especially as the increase of indirect taxes often further crippled the humbler subject at the same time as it reached his superiors.

Henry IV and Louis XIII

Henri IV gained his kingdom by degrees. Named as heir by the dying Henri III in 1589, deprived by the hand of death of his closest rival for the throne, the Cardinal de Bourbon, in 1590, he returned to the true faith of the Catholic Church in 1593, and finally entered his capital in

1594, conspicuously refraining from taking revenge on those who had opposed him. The League was in disarray, with its allies drastically depleted, and many of its members therefore decided to support the king in his attempt to establish internal peace, whatever religious disunity remained. When Henri declared war on Spain in 1595, which ended with what was, for France, the desirable Treaty of Vervins in 1598, he had the backing of most of the French nation. Now, with his great minister Sully, the restoration of the kingdom could begin.

Many of the royal ministers of the seventeenth century shared common aims, even if they achieved varying degrees of success in pursuing them. They sought to introduce expert knowledge into the administrative machinery and to direct it more closely from the centre, to inquire into and systematize the use of the country's resources, and to replace the many different provincial standards of taxation, justice, weights and measures by nationally acceptable codes and tables. In economics there were the tasks of uniting the disparate provinces into a viable whole, of improving tax assessment and collection, of reducing or avoiding fiscal exemptions, and of planning royal expenditure so that the ministers were not having perpetual recourse to short-term emergency taxation as a way of meeting unforeseen expenses. There was the permanent fear of war, which always threw the royal finances into crisis, and there was the Huguenot community which, if it were docile in 1598, could not but alarm ministers who remembered the religious wars in their own country and saw similar conflicts continuing elsewhere.

The rise of more expert, professional administrators could be clearly seen in the central government before the accession of Henri IV, but it was to be a very slow process to introduce them into provincial and municipal institutions. At the centre the secretaries of state continued to accumulate power during the first half of the seventeenth century, even though their influence declined at times. The secretary of state was one of the 'new men' whom French kings frequently employed, hoping to reinvigorate the administration by placing a newly and rapidly promoted servant, and therefore a grateful one, in authority over selfish office-holders. Louis XI and François I had tried this remedy, but each new layer of men became just one further stratum in the bureaucracy, as self-seeking as the rest.

Under the great ministers who dominated French government from 1598 until 1661 – Sully, Richelieu and Mazarin – the secretaries were influential members of the central conciliar system, loyally carrying out their duties and forming a kind of inner cabinet in which they gave constant advice. The ministers and secretaries screened the king from the public in the sense that they took the blame for unpopular policies, and preserved the integrity of the crown. Although Louis XIII by no means relinquished all power into Richelieu's hands, the young Louis XIV was nevertheless hailed as the monarch who came to save France after a half century of ministerial tyranny. But when, on Mazarin's death in 1661, he made a point of underlining his determination to be his own first minister, the policies continued unchanged, except that they could be prosecuted more fiercely now that they were the personal wishes of a divinely ordained monarch. Kings and ministers alike believed in a State whose interests overrode all others, and to whose greater glory all personal considerations must be sacrificed. The inhabitants of provincial France found the resulting policies bewildering, for the good of the State was seldom compatible with their own advancement.

The ministry of Colbert (1661–83) saw the greatest progress in the reform of finance, the economy and the administration, but the ground had already been laid by his predecessors. Sully wrestled with the finances after the civil wars, although the economic state of the country was not so bad as is sometimes claimed, and introduced some kind of budgeting, even if the reliability of these forecasts of State expenditure declined during the regency for Louis XIII. Sully is to be praised more for his plans to order the finances and the bureaucracy than for his success. Foreign policy and defence had to be given priority, but his schemes for the clearer delineation of France's frontiers, the building of a large fleet, the expansion of the economy, the construction of roads, bridges and canals, the accurate assessment of the resources of the country, and, above all, the establishment of a powerful monarchy, at the head of a national Church, free from the independent power of nobles who plotted against ministers like himself, and supported by a bureaucracy which served the interests of the crown in preference to its own – all these aims were to be adopted by his successors.

A noticeable characteristic of the first quarter of the seventeenth century was a more general revival of interest in economics. A number of pamphlets and learned works, of which Montchrestien's *Traicté de l'œconomie politique* (1615) was only the most distinguished, proposed the expansion of trade, the development of industry and reform of taxation. All these writers, like the ministers themselves, built their plans more or less closely around the mercantilist principles which were evolving during the sixteenth century and were to influence France for more than another hundred years. Believing that France was rich in natural resources and potentially self-sufficient, they wished to keep gold and silver within the kingdom, to manufacture at home all those luxury goods which could be bought only at great expense from abroad, to expand industry, to employ the workless poor and to promulgate regulations for controlling every aspect of the economy. They particularly directed their propaganda at the Estates-General of 1614 and the Assembly of Notables of 1626, hoping that these bodies would pronounce in favour of the plans which the government had formulated. However, their assumption that France was a natural economic unit, whose frontiers could be clearly delineated by tariffs, was at variance with the provincialism of the country. Many provinces did not share these beliefs of the writers and ministers, certain of them feeling closer commercially to other countries than to some of their fellow Frenchmen.

Henri IV and Sully therefore concentrated on those of their reform plans which involved less of an attack on local privilege, namely the development of crafts and luxury goods, and of a share in the trade between Europe and the new colonial world. Trading companies were formed, and an attempt made at providing State protection for merchants. They did not feel strong enough to undertake the overhaul of the fiscal system, and France still lagged behind her competitors in consequence. Her fleet was poor, she lacked skilled workers, her industrial products were expensive and she was lying well back in the colonial race.

Not every example of opposition to royal economic and financial policy on the part of the office-holders can be explained simply by their corrupt natures. On some occasions the relevant officials could not raise the required revenues. But far too often they were disinclined to co-operate. It was impossible thoroughly to supervise whether royal orders were executed properly, and although Sully attacked a few flagrant instances of corruption or reluctance to obey the commands of the crown, the effort and expense involved prevented an investigation into all but this extreme fringe. Worst of all, by authorizing the establishment of the *Paulette* in 1604, he permitted, for the financial benefit of the treasury, the creation by royal edict of a hereditary bureaucracy, before which time venality had merely been permitted by custom alone.

During the ministry of Sully the sovereign courts – the *parlements*, *chambres des comptes, cours des aides* and *cour des monnaies* – began more and more systematically to put forward their own views, frequently in opposition to the wishes of the crown. The king in France was the unlimited author of law, but he relied on these courts to register his edicts and to dispense his justice. In return they were beginning first to be obstructive and soon to make positive demands on him. At the same time the central government was making irregular use of the *commissaire*, forerunner of the *intendant*, an official sent out by the king to investigate specific grievances and instances of maladministration, and reporting back to Paris. The *commissaires* were to become crucial targets of odium for the courts in their struggle with the royal ministers which culminated in the Fronde.

Sully fell from power soon after the assassination of Henri IV in 1610, and his successors quickly squandered the surplus funds he had left in the treasury. But the problems remained – the fear of Habsburg encirclement was growing, the nobility were still too dangerous, the finances were inadequate and the bureaucracy over-powerful, while the perils of a Protestant State within the realm seemed ever more alarming.

The Huguenots were a very difficult problem. With the memory of recent civil war in France, and the evidence of lasting religious conflict in other countries, few Frenchmen could regard the question of toleration objectively. The majority hoped for a more permanent solution than had been possible at the end of the sixteenth century. The *politique* party, mild Catholics who wished to put the peace of the kingdom before religion, had triumphed with the Edict of Nantes in 1598, which gave the Huguenots a considerable degree of security in political, administrative, financial, economic, military and religious matters. The Protestant nobles and their coreligionaries in the towns were prepared to defend these rights with vigour, but the slow attack on their religion began almost as soon as the Edict was signed and registered. Sully, himself a Protestant, was no advocate of them as candidates for high office. He, like any patriotic Frenchman, knew that a tolerant peace had been unavoidable, but that further integration of the faiths was unwise. As Henri IV showed increasing hostility towards his former religion, under the influence of his Jesuit confessor, the government began to exert pressure on this minority, offering every encouragement to converts and distributing no favour to those who remained staunchly Protestant. The Huguenots saw their numbers and their territory declining, but the wealth of their towns was sufficient to sustain their military strength. After Henri IV was killed in 1610, the kingdom was entrusted to the pro-Spanish and zealous Catholic Queen Mother, Marie de' Medici, and her favourites, which divided the Huguenot party. Their towns chose to remain loyal to the Regent, while their nobility joined forces with rebellious Catholic nobles. The Huguenot aristocracy supported any group which challenged the authority of the crown. Initially opposing the Queen Mother, they championed her cause after her disgrace and turned their hatred against the new minister, the Duc de Luynes. Louis XIII and Luynes were preparing for an attack on the Protestants, which they launched in 1620, and religious conflict raged during 1621 and 1622. The royal army was by no means the unqualified victor, especially as Luynes himself died during the campaign.

The leader of the revolt of the Catholic nobles, which the Huguenot nobility joined, was the Prince de Condé, son of the Condé who had featured prominently in the civil wars. Condé failed to win the important support of the *parlement* of Paris for his cause, because he had attacked the venal bureaucracy and demanded its destruction in an attempt to widen the ranks of his followers, and the movement failed. He was arrested in 1616, but in 1622 he and the disgraced Queen Mother were back in the circle of advisers around the king, which deprived them of some grounds for opposing royal policies. Only twice removed from succession to the throne of the childless king, Condé personified the power of a prince of the blood at its most dangerous. Moreover, during these disturbances the Thirty Years War was breaking out in Europe near every French frontier, and the strength of the French crown and that of the various anti-royalist parties was related to the complicated manœuvrings in European diplomacy. The Huguenots, fearing an alliance between France and their own most likely ally, England, even wooed their opposite number in religion, zealously Catholic Spain. The intertwining of national and international politics which had occurred during the later sixteenth century was again to be seen. After another Huguenot rising in 1625 the new minister, Richelieu, made a temporary peace with them in 1626, but the problem of religion remained unsolved.

1626 is a convenient moment to gauge the reactions of French society to the economic and religious policies of the preceding quarter century because in that year an Assembly of Notables was called which, like the Estates-General of 1614, revealed the attitudes of various social groups. At the Estates-General, meeting for the last time before 1789, a number of the problems confronting the crown were discussed. The Third Estate wanted peace through a strengthened central authority, a firmer attack on the Huguenots, the reform of military pay in order to prevent looting by the soldiery, the compelling of the able-bodied poor to work and the reduction of pensions paid to the nobility. The noble Estate deplored the increasing bureaucratic element within their class. All three Estates attacked luxury and the amount of money which left the kingdom to pay for luxury goods from abroad.

The Estates-General was not mourned when it lapsed in 1614. It had lost its powers of consenting to taxation, and its component Estates found it difficult to evolve opinions which were shared by all their members from the varied provinces of France. The surviving provincial Estates were more dynamic as they provided a forum in which the representatives of a more viable geographical unit could air their views and grievances, having also the right to vote certain taxes and to control much local administration and expenditure, which strengthened their hand in dealing with the central government. On the national level, the mood of the country was a little more clearly seen in the Assemblies of Notables, summoned for the last time in 1626 until 1788. After 1626, French kings relied for advice on royal councils and on personal friends.

The Assemblies were composed of specially invited nobles and clergy, who spoke as individuals and not on behalf of their order as was the case at the Estates-General, together with the *premiers présidents* and *procureurs-généraux* of the sovereign courts who did speak as representatives of their colleagues. Richelieu hoped that a decision by the Assembly would therefore bind the courts to act accordingly. The 1626 meeting expressed its belief in the economic strength of France, the need for a larger fleet and for the development of colonial companies, insisting however that the edicts establishing such companies be registered by the *parlements*, in the knowledge that those courts would use their right of remonstrance against them. Beyond that the nobles and officials each managed to nullify a number of proposals aimed at their own authority. The nobles complained again about the new nobility of office-holders, the officials insisted on the confirmation of all their past rights in administration and justice, the clergy clashed with the militant religious nationalism of the *parlements*. The overall effect was completely to wreck Richelieu's hopes for financial reform.

From this moment, the *parlements* and other members of the *robe* increased their opposition to the attempts of the royal ministers at relieving the ever worsening financial situation. Nor were other opponents silent. In 1626 Richelieu was the target of the conspiracy of Chalais, when a group of great nobles, including a number of princes of the blood, sought to dislodge him in answer to his efforts towards dismissing Montmorency from his position as Admiral of France, one of the high offices which gave powerful individuals an excessive degree of independent control over important aspects of government. The conspiracy failed, the post was abolished, and the corresponding rank in the army, the Constable, was suppressed in the same year on the death of its holder, the Duc de Lesdiguières.

Thus were the policies of Sully continued by Luynes and Richelieu. A last onslaught on the Huguenots, with the capture of their crucial port of La Rochelle, ended the conflict in 1629, and although many Protestants remained in France, their independent power was crushed. Further colonial ventures failed in seas now full of warships as well as pirates, and the struggle with the Habsburgs, so long awaited and prepared for, was imminent. The problem of financing it was a desperate one. The squandering of the surplus left by Sully and inadequate budgeting under the Regency had led to the raising of forced loans from royal officials, and in the 1620s to the creation of more offices for sale. Most of the resulting profits went on the army and on campaigns against the Huguenots, and a sizeable sum on pensions to the nobility. Already the government was anticipating the revenues of the following year, in order to balance its accounts.

During the minority the crown began to rely for revenue on a new social group, which also started to infiltrate into the bureaucracy – the financiers. These men had made their fortunes in the world of money and credit, and were often the tax-farmers who collected indirect taxation for the State, eventually buying themselves an office. Sully had obliged the tax-farmers to abandon their commercial interests, which conflicted with their priorities as collectors of revenue, and they therefore devoted themselves exclusively to finance. All indirect taxes were farmed out at public auctions to the highest bidder, who then appointed agents to collect the money for him to pay into the treasury. Even though the returns fluctuated with the economic state of the country, tax-farming was a profitable business at which men made quick fortunes, although until they purchased an office they lacked the security of tenure of the bureaucrat, which made it easier for the crown to obtain forced loans from them. If the system was unsatisfactory, it was beyond the power of ministers to change it, and at least the crown was borrowing from its own agents instead of from the independent and even foreign bankers on whom it had depended in the past.

Despite these problems, Richelieu was in a strong position. The year after the Protestant challenge had been finally repelled, the 'Day of Dupes' conspiracy removed the Queen Mother from her position of influence over her son. If there were further aristocratic attempts to unseat him, his survival in the king's favour was never really in doubt again. Until this moment he had not allowed France to enter the Thirty Years War, although he was subsidizing the Protestant Gustavus Adolphus of Sweden who was fighting to secure the same ends. Religious differences did not bother Richelieu greatly in choosing allies. When Sweden fared badly in 1634, Richelieu prepared for direct intervention and declared war in 1635, a conflict which was to last in Germany until 1648, and against Spain until 1659. The minister was left with little time to spare for the internal problems of France, and on his death in 1642 bequeathed them and the war to his successor as minister, Mazarin, a cardinal like himself, and to the five-year-old boy who in 1643 succeeded his father as Louis XIV.

One further aspect of life under the first two Bourbons must be mentioned – the development of the Catholic Church, apart from the Huguenot question. Protestantism was not the only religious issue during these years. The forces of Counter-Reformation Catholicism were active throughout Europe, and the memory of extreme Catholic partisans in the civil war was just as disquieting to the central government as their recollections of Calvinist dissidence. The king was effective head of the Church in France and divinely installed upon the throne, although royal and papal publicists argued passionately in the first years of the century about the theoretical basis of his sovereignty. So too the clergy at the Estates-General and at the Assembly of Notables preferred a less aggressive Gallicanism to that advocated by other groups, especially by the *parlements*. The *parlements* vigorously opposed the decision of Henri IV to readmit the Jesuits to France, but the king, with his influential Jesuit confessor, was now a true son of the Roman Church, working for ends of which the Pope himself approved. This co-operation became closer under the zealously Catholic regency of Marie de' Medici, when national policy was altered to suit the interests of the Church.

In the countryside the Church was playing a different role. The revived fervour of Catholicism was directed towards, among other things, the problem of the poor. Charitable associations were formed, such as the Companies of the Holy Sacrament, dedicated to creating poor-houses in which the needy could be imprisoned and compelled to work usefully, for this charity was not kindly and warm-hearted. Thus a potentially dangerous element on the urban scene was safely contained. People of all classes joined these charitable enterprises, working anonymously in order to appear more selfless. The government suspected such secret societies, just as it feared the purposes of the men, often of high *robe* nobility, who entered that other mysterious religious brotherhood – the Jansenists. Secrecy and extreme zeal, especially religious zeal, were all too frequently associated with treason.

Only a small percentage of the poor benefited from these charities during the reign of Louis XIII, and poverty was widespread all over France where it gave rise to frequent local revolts. The Fronde of 1648 was simply the culmination of a series of separate insurrections which had punctuated the preceding thirty years, and even earlier centuries, revolts which were often incited by privileged members of society but in which the hungry formed the bulk of the rebels. The peasant, torn between the fiscal demands made on him by the crown on the one hand and by his *seigneur* on the other, tended to support these local and more personally relevant forces against the agents from distant Paris. Sometimes it was the local courts or the municipal authorities who stirred up trouble – anyone in fact except the merchants, for whom revolt meant the disruption of business. Such insurrections were largely short-term attacks on specific grievances, usually fiscal. They had no genuinely revolutionary characteristics, and were quick to subside either when a royal army was said to be approaching or when the temporary distress of plague or a bad harvest had been followed by a more prosperous season in which the tax burden seemed a little less than unbearable. The Frenchman could sincerely cry 'Long live the King, but without taxation'.

Louis XIV

Mazarin, first minister from 1642 until his death in 1661, inherited formidable problems, though he might at least have derived some comfort from the defeat of the Spanish army at Rocroi when the new reign was but a few days old. In addition to the burden of war, the chaotic royal finances, the large venal bureaucracy and the stubborn opposition of privileged groups in society, he now had to defeat the reviving ambitions of the princes of the blood, for whom a long minor-

ity meant a chance to seize supreme authority. The Regent – the Queen
Mother, Anne of Austria – and Mazarin found these challenges all-
absorbing, and allowed commercial life to stagnate. The superintendent
of finances, Nicolas Fouquet, gave some stimulus to commerce in the
later 1650s, and was the moving spirit behind the improved poor-
relief of that decade, but for Mazarin himself commerce was interesting
only in so far as it brought in revenue. Therefore the cardinal was keen
to raise tariffs but reluctant to spend money on the navy. One of the
few signs that the traditional economic rules were being observed was
the promulgation of laws against luxury, but this simply served to
offend the growing ostentation of the bourgeoisie and nobility.

In 1648 Mazarin's foreign policy reached a high point with the ending of the Thirty Years War by the Peace of Westphalia, but that
acted almost as a signal for a wave of fresh disturbances within the
kingdom. There have been many conflicting interpretations of the
Frondes, because the Frondeurs seem to have been composed of so
many different groups, whose unity was short-lived and whose sole
common emotion appears to have been their hatred for the Italian
cardinal. He was now the target of an enormous number of satires and
slanders which were being widely circulated – the 'Mazarinades'. It is
true that the whole realm was affected by the war, the ruinous level
of taxation, the extra subsidies and the passage of troops across the
countryside, but beyond this point the complaints diverged. The
greatest nobles hoped to replace Mazarin in the centre of power; the
seigneurs found that the peasants could not afford to pay their feudal
dues in addition to the royal taxes; those who had lent money to the
State, especially the humbler townsmen who had invested in royal
bonds (*rentes*), feared for their investments as the government became
increasingly impoverished; the sovereign courts objected to the attempts by the cardinal to force them to register unpopular edicts, while
the lesser office-holders were concerned for their offices; the peasants
simply wished to avoid the starvation which followed from the co-
incidence of high taxes and bad harvests. The crown was in the hands
of the financiers and could not free itself, and it needed only the Peace
of Westphalia to release those criticisms which had been partly suppressed during the Thirty Years War, even though the Spanish war
was still continuing.

The rallying cries of the Frondeurs did not correspond to all these
grievances. The loudest claims were voiced by the *parlement* of Paris,
which became a self-appointed tribune for other groups in society who

would normally have regarded its friendship with suspicion. In particular the *parlement* championed the financial officials in their opposition to the royal *intendants* in the provinces, whose dismissal was one of the principal demands made by the Frondeurs. The *intendants* or *commissaires* had existed since the sixteenth century, though their irregular visits had lengthened over the years. Richelieu had used them, but not excessively. The royal officials therefore were complaining not so much that these agents of the central bureaucracy were undermining their powers at the moment, but rather that they feared the usurpation of their authority in the future. It was ironic, of course, that the post of *intendant* was now a recognized step in the hierarchy of promotion within the *noblesse de robe*, and that many who disliked this kind of official would have been willing to accept such a post for themselves.

The most remarkable manifestation of the newly found *robe* solidarity was the pact of union of 13 May 1648, when all the sovereign courts of Paris joined forces and met during the following month in the Chambre de Saint-Louis, to put forward their demands for the reform of abuses. At the same time, other levels of the bureaucracy were submitting their grievances too. The courts demanded that all administration be carried out by the proper permanent officials, that the *intendants* be withdrawn immediately and that the conditions of office-holding be confirmed and safeguarded. The *Paulette* had been suspended briefly on previous occasions since its establishment in 1604, and the office-holders perpetually feared that the crown might do so again, thereby abrogating their right to bequeath their offices to their heirs. Making the fatal mistake of arresting the popular *parlementaire* Broussel, the Regent saw the barricades rise in Paris. In the first days of 1649 she was forced to take the little king by night from his capital, where he could not be said to be safe in his own palace because of the menaces of his angry people, much as they loved him personally. Thus in January 1649 the Fronde began, the *parlementaires* being led by some of the greatest nobles who soon showed themselves unconcerned about the views of the courts and preoccupied instead with establishing their own authority which, needless to say, they claimed to exercise on behalf of a king who was evilly counselled by wicked ministers. As Condé and the royal troops advanced, the *parlement* decided that its princely allies were too unreliable and made peace at Rueil on 11 March 1649.

The parlementary Fronde was over, but the longer Fronde of the princes lay ahead. From 1650 until 1652 this conflict raged throughout France, usually stimulated by the highest aristocrats, and leaving misery in many areas which had experienced a bad harvest in 1649 and now suffered another in 1651. Mazarin found it expeditious to leave the country on two occasions, but still retained control of the government. Condé turned his allegiance to the princely side, the *parlement* again flirted with the princes and was again disillusioned, and the struggle ended with the arrest of the leading rebels who were members of the royal and other distinguished noble houses. The bourgeoisie in many towns remained loyal, if disgruntled, while the poorer townsmen often supported the risings. Mazarin had been compelled to recall the *intendants*, but he had no intention of respecting for one day longer than necessary the promises extracted from him by the *parlement*. Thus ended the Frondes, a series of protests by reactionary groups, each trying to safeguard its own position and lacking any kind of revolutionary or reforming policies. Unlike the disturbances in certain other European countries in the middle years of the seventeenth century, which some recent historians have tried to explain by a general theory,[1] the Frondes included no significant group which wanted to acquire powers it had never possessed. In France such groups were rather defending their existing powers, and traditional paths had already been created by which the ambitious could gain influence. There was no need or cause for revolution.

In the later 1650s the country was tired of civil and international war, and Mazarin wooed the *parlement* of Paris at the same time as he was putting his own trusted servants into important positions in the government – men like Colbert, the future chancellor Le Tellier, Lionne and Fouquet, the great ministerial names of the personal rule of Louis XIV. Mazarin was restored to full power under a king whose majority had been declared, so that a rebel could no longer claim that he was fighting for a minor king who was being misled by wicked ministers. Throughout the Frondes the Huguenots had remained firmly loyal, no doubt because many were traders who shared Catholic middle-class resentment at the disruption of commerce by war. Also they took great care to dissociate themselves from the behaviour of their coreligionaries in England, whose murder of their rightful and God-given king horrified Frenchmen.

Meanwhile the war with Spain dragged on and the royal finances were still in a deplorable state. When the Treaty of the Pyrenees ended the conflict in 1659, and friendship was cemented by the marriage of

---

[1] See the articles contained in T. Aston, op. cit.

Louis XIV to a Spanish bride in 1660, Mazarin could justly pride himself on concluding a war which had finally broken the threat of Habsburg encirclement of France on the Spanish and imperial frontiers; but the expenses of these campaigns had prevented him from attempting any major financial reforms, and the confusion which he bequeathed to his successors was serious indeed.

When in 1661 Louis XIV declared that he would rule without a first minister, there began a period for which a great deal of documentary evidence survives, far more than for preceding years. These rich funds of source material are vital for the historian, because they reveal the practical limitations on royal power which are not easily perceived from a study of the plans and pronouncements of the king and his ministers. The personal rule was a long struggle between reforming ministers and reactionary society.

How far can the government of Louis XIV be described as 'absolute'? As was said above, royal authority was widely thought to have a clearly defined sphere of influence, and within its bounds no one thought to challenge the king. The princes might try to displace a minister in order to surround the monarch with advisers of aristocratic outlook, although Louis was determined that they should not influence his personal rule, but not even they could seriously hope to limit the royal power of decision. Nor were there any bodies who could be said to speak on behalf of the nation. Yet the authority of the king was limited in fact. Although Louis XIV intended to govern without a minister to replace Mazarin, preferring instead to make decisions in small councils of highly favoured secretaries, and although these councils relied on the *intendants* for detailed information about the situation in the provinces, the policies evolved in the central councils and approved by the king had to be implemented by the monolithic venal bureaucracy. Here were ample opportunities for men to delay royal orders, especially as the *intendant*, who was supposed to supervise the work of the officials and report delinquents, was often too busy to watch closely over them. Many royal decisions were reiterated more than once over the years, because they were being only partially carried out in the localities. When the *intendants* came to be more widely used under Colbert, the government received more reliable information but without a corresponding improvement in the machinery by which policies were enacted. Moreover in the *pays d'états* the provincial Estates controlled much of the administration within the province as of right, while municipal authorities throughout France had a considerable degree of independence. The battle between central government and local privilege was far from being decided.

1661 brought little change to the upper levels of government. The new ministers – Le Tellier, Fouquet, Lionne and Colbert – were all trusted servants of the cardinal and came from *noblesse de robe* families of no great antiquity, often being decried as 'bourgeois' by their detractors. Every one of them was an expert administrator. Fouquet, the superintendent of finances, was soon removed from their ranks, being arrested in September 1661 and finally disgraced after a long trial in 1664, because the independent wealth he had acquired made him a positive threat to the king. Louis XIV intended that he himself should be seen to be sole master of his kingdom, the ruler whom the people were demanding in the 1650s as their saviour from ministerial tyranny and as the reincarnation of the great Henri IV. They did not realize at first that little had altered, and that the Le Tellier family and Colbert were nearly as hateful as Mazarin. Within the new councils Louis XIV personally made the decisions, but was of course dependent entirely on the material which his ministers put before him. This is not to say that they regularly tried to mislead him, but the increasing volume of routine state business was too vast for one person to supervise. A man of unremarkable intelligence, the king nevertheless laboured long hours with his ministers and secretaries of state at the ever more complicated tasks which lay in front of them, attempting to apply the principle that every important action of his administrators should have been approved first in these central councils.

Louis XIV still had close aristocratic friends whom he trusted and frequently asked for advice, particularly if they held that one important office which could be given only to a great noble who was also an intimate of the monarch – a provincial governorship. In those provinces that were far from Paris and had turbulent local Estates, a powerful aristocratic governor, usually with lands in the area and with effective influence through clientage, was an essential agent of the crown if royal policies were to be successfully accepted by the people. He might be aided by an *intendant*, about whose appointment he would often have been consulted. The difference between those provinces which were administered by an effective governor and those which were supervised solely by an *intendant* was that the former had a champion who, while he was devoted to executing the commands of the crown, would also defend their interests and plead on their behalf to the king. Louis XIV often listened sympathetically to these reports from his noble friends. The *intendant*, in contrast, tended to regard everything with the eye of the central government, and was not infrequently rebuked by the royal ministers for exceeding his authority and for disregarding the regulations which limited his own power and preserved the rights and powers of others.

Great claims have been made for the *intendants* as agents of so-called absolute monarchy, especially when Colbert made them into permanent and resident officials, drafted to an area in which they had no personal connections and therefore impervious to local interests and pressures. This is too simplified a picture. The *intendants* came from the ranks of the *robe* and hoped to return to a higher post within them. In an effort to accelerate their promotion and escape from virtual exile in a remote district, they sometimes distorted the situation in their province, telling the central government what it wished to hear and making their own administration seem more successful. As their tasks multiplied, they were forced to rely on the services of *sub-délégués*, helpers who were natives of the area in which they worked and involved in local affairs, and the *intendant* might himself decide to co-operate with local interests as well. Even if he were scrupulous, he could not hope to scrutinize all aspects of administration within his region every year, particularly as his only way of checking corruption in the fiscal system was to inspect all aspects of the process, from the interrogation of every humble taxpayer to the auditing of the accounts of the various strata of collectors. He did not replace existing officials, but simply observed their conduct and reported on it to Paris. Moreover the crown was reluctant to give him general powers, preferring to authorize him to take specific action against specific abuses on which he had reported to the royal council. It is true that the *intendant* made some improvement in the system of administration, but only by exposing and punishing the most flagrant examples of corruption in the hope that others, less corrupt, would take fright and behave a little more honourably. In a difficult situation and a hostile area, the sole means by which the *intendant* could enforce the orders of the king was by calling out the royal troops – and this itself had a disruptive effect on society because of the disorders which always attended the passage of the army, not to mention the fact that there were insufficient soldiers to permit regular administration by this method and that they and their officers could not always be wholly relied on.

There could be no question of replacing the venal bureaucracy by an alternative system. Colbert tried hard in the 1660s to reduce surplus offices, although his success in doing so was eventually undermined by the creation of further offices to help finance expensive wars. Yet the method of instilling fear into the many by punishment of the few worked satisfactorily within limits. The disgrace of Fouquet alarme d people, as did the occasional exile of members of sovereign courts who were being unusually obstreperous. In 1661 a *chambre de justice* was created to investigate all financial abuses, and terrified corrupt financiers and officials before it was abolished in 1669 on the grounds that it was causing more ill-feeling than it was producing benefits. Judicial officials were even more harassed by the special royal inquests in the provinces, the *Grands Jours*, that in the notoriously corrupt province of Auvergne in 1665 inspired terror among the privileged classes. Such demonstrations, because of their vigour and disruptive effect, could also be used only occasionally and to set an example. Longer-term reform of the system was needed.

Although Colbert tried to stamp out corruption in the bureaucracy, that did not solve one problem – namely that the jurisdictions of various officials overlapped, so that some might reverse the decisions of others, though all were acting legally and within their rights. The most serious clashes occurred between the *intendants* and certain of the law courts. For example the *intendants* acquired the right to adjust the allocation of taxes by on the spot impositions, but the taxpayer was then entitled to appeal against this new assessment to the *cour des aides*. All too often the court allowed the appeal.

The courts and officials were in a strong position. In France there had never been a distinction between the judiciary and the executive. Each branch of the administrative hierarchy dealt with infringements of its own regulations. It was therefore difficult to win a case against an official, as he was part of the system whose own court heard the charge. Because of the hierarchy of courts through which a case might travel, together with the slowness and the cost of litigation, many people never bothered to initiate legal proceedings. If the king was unlimited in his power to make law, he had to rely on these venal office-holders of the courts to administer it. Although in 1673 the *parlements* lost their right to remonstrate against edicts before they registered them, having henceforward to register them first and remonstrate afterwards, they still had considerable power to delay the execution of many royal decrees by allowing the appeals of litigants in cases which were brought to them for judgement. Colbert's reforms undoubtedly improved the situation, and made officials afraid of going too far in opposition to royal orders, but the reforms often seem more impressive on paper than they were in reality. Thus the great codification of French law – the Civil Ordinance of 1667, the Regulations for Waters and Forests of 1669, the Criminal Code of 1670, the Commercial Ordinance of 1673, the Naval Ordinance of 1681 and the Black Code on slavery and colonies in 1685 – did reduce the conflicts in jurisdictions and the variants in local practice, and some of these codes formed the basis of French law until the nineteenth century, but in the seventeenth century, from the moment these ordinances were promulgated, there were frequent complaints that some of their specific provisions were being habitually disregarded and infringements going unpunished. All these codes imposed heavier penalties for corruption and breaches of royal regulations than had been decreed in the past, but also removed the death penalty from those crimes which offended superstition rather than reason.

The burning problem for the French crown in 1661 was financial, and it was tackled rapidly and successfully by Colbert. This was doubly necessary because, no matter how meagre the resources in the treasury, Louis was always prepared to spend lavishly on his court and on the other physical manifestations of royal authority, expenditure which the loyal and patriotic Colbert was ever willing to condone. The 1660s saw a number of attempts to increase the revenue of the crown, and to tap other reservoirs of wealth in the realm which escaped the burden of taxation. Unfortunately, the years of financial exploitation under Richelieu and Mazarin had bred a strong mistrust of government intentions, and some schemes accordingly cancelled each other out. For example, Colbert investigated the legitimacy of noble titles, in order to prove who was not truly noble and therefore not eligible for tax exemption. On the other hand he annulled the laws forbidding nobles to enter seaborne trade, in the hope of persuading them to join his new colonial companies. Many aristocrats, apart from the disdain they felt for commerce, linked the two policies and feared they were being tricked into forfeiting their nobility by entering commerce and being declared commoners.

Colbert was very well aware of the massive fiscal burden which fell on the humbler subjects of Louis XIV. Accordingly his policy was to decrease direct taxes and increase indirect levies which fell on a wider range of people. Also he hoped that a much-publicized reduction in direct taxation would encourage foreign investment in a France which thus appeared to be in a stronger financial position. It should not be thought that the government was motivated by a genuine human concern for the peasant – it was simply that extreme action against them, like the seizure of their livestock as payment for outstanding taxes, deprived them of their livelihood and prevented them from paying taxes in subsequent years. So too Colbert sought to stop the widespread imprisonment of the local, elected collectors of the direct taxes for failing to extract these dues from a poor peasantry, as it deprived them of the opportunity to collect anything at all and was harmful to the interests of the state. At least the indirect taxes could be farmed out to financiers, whose fortunes could be unscrupulously exploited by the royal ministers without endangering their survival.

In the *pays d'états* the Estates had the right to dispute the exact amount of direct taxes to be levied within the province. This gave rise to lengthy bargaining in which the Estates demanded the preservation of provincial privileges as the price which the crown had to pay for much-needed revenues. Such methods were accepted practice, the king requesting too large a sum, the province offering too little, after which the noble governor and others used all their influence and patronage behind the scenes to bring about an eventual compromise. The Estates had sole responsibility for allocating the tax burden within that area and, ironically, based their assessment on fairer principles and more detailed information than was possible in the *pays d'élections*, for in the former the actual resources of the taxpayers were estimated whereas in the latter the allocation was on a *per capita* basis. Colbert tried to extend the more detailed method to the whole country, but it proved impossible to gather sufficient information to make it viable. The *pays d'états*, for all their opposition, privileges and pride, were in many senses more efficiently administered than the other provinces.

The expansion of commerce was the means by which Colbert hoped to bring about the greatest improvement in French finance, although these policies received only cursory support from a king who preferred to think of wars and glory. The problem was twofold. There was the need to increase the French share of trade between western Europe and the colonies, and there was the equally vital task of abolishing the numerous privileges and regulations which hampered trade within the kingdom. Even the colonial trade affected local rights, by giving monopolies to certain ports at the expense of others. Colbert was more successful than his predecessors in attracting investors to his colonial companies, but too many wealthy men still preferred to purchase office or, if they were noble already, to follow the traditional and extravagant life of the aristocrat. A few nobles were becoming involved in commerce, but they were outnumbered by commoners who abandoned their business interests on joining the bureaucracy. The obsession with social prestige still restricted economic advance.

Colbert followed the mercantilist principles which earlier ministers and their advisers had observed throughout the seventeenth century, but this too provoked hostility in the provinces. Because of internal customs barriers, especially the heavy duties on goods crossing the boundaries of the *cinq grosses fermes* (the customs area which comprised most of northern France), some provinces concentrated on trading with other countries, paying less dues than when they traded with their own capital. Although Colbert simplified the tariffs of the *cinq grosses fermes*, the problem remained, and when he began to wage a tariff war against the Dutch, he was attacking the regular commercial partner of a province like Brittany which was outside the *cinq grosses fermes*. Many other national policies conflicted with the interests of the varied and separate provinces in the further reaches of the kingdom, partly because the merchants were not always the most objective and far-sighted of traders. In Marseille their concern was always to keep control of all commerce which passed through the port, deliberately sabotaging attempts to attract the ships of other countries which would have benefited France as a whole. Despite constant encouragement of ship-building, in which there was admittedly an improvement, the French lagged far behind the Dutch and the English.

Louis approved Colbert's hatred of the Dutch, if for different reasons, To Colbert they had an unfair share of European trade, to the king they were Protestants and republicans. Their agreed solution was to destroy them. At other times during his ministry, Colbert found himself at loggerheads with the bellicose war minister Louvois, son of Le Tellier, resenting the drain imposed by such hostilities on the revenues he was painstakingly accumulating. But for the Dutch War he was eager. Had he known that it was to last from 1672 until 1678 and cause him to reintroduce short-term means of raising money which he had spent much of his first ten years in abolishing, he might have been less enthusiastic.

Although Colbert reorganized the customs dues of the *cinq grosses fermes*, he failed to reduce the many tariffs on road and river routes throughout the rest of France. He did sponsor schemes for new bridges and canals, notably that for the Canal du Languedoc which was to connect the Atlantic with the Mediterranean, but once again the royal administration proved inadequate to supervise such projects. They were therefore entrusted to private individuals, who were allowed to impose a new toll on the completed route to recompense themselves. In much of France the crown would make a grant towards the most important of these works, but in the *pays d'états*, which the king considered to be undertaxed, almost the whole financial burden was laid on the provincial Estates themselves.

Colbert also speeded industrial development, although he concentrated chiefly on producing within France industrial products which normally came from abroad. To this end he encouraged the immigration of foreign craftsmen, tried to mobilize the poor, established stern regulations about quality, attempted with little success to standardize weights and measures and advocated the expansion of mining. He was not alone in following this course, and it is interesting to note that he received relevant information about further opportunities for industrial growth not only from the *intendants*, but also from the aristocratic governors of Brittany, Boulogne and Burgundy. These great nobles, the last named being none other than the Prince de Condé, sent him detailed reports on existing manufactures and proposed new ventures, while the governor of Lyon introduced pilot schemes for foreign luxury goods on his own estates.[1] If many Frenchmen despised the world of commerce and industry, there were also influential supporters of an economic revival.

The municipalities were another serious problem. Elected councillors and mayors, although the latter were increasingly royal nominees, flagrancy abused their powers. Many towns had become heavily in debt and, despite Colbert's attempts to free them from this burden, continued to squander funds needlessly. As they were responsible for financing public works within their walls, for providing forces of law and order, and for sanitation and street-cleaning, such matters were often neglected. Town life could be filthy and dangerous. Many town councils were in the hands of established families who showed little concern for the interests of other citizens, especially for those of the merchants. Once again the *intendant* could recommend the punishment

[1] The governors illustrate admirably the dangers of studying only the pronouncements of the king and the ministers, without examining individual examples. The king decreed that governors should be appointed for only three years at a time, thereby giving him an opportunity to unseat those who proved unsatisfactory. Yet in a number of provinces, mostly *pays d'états*, great nobles who were trusted friends of the monarch, and often their descendants too, held a governorship for years and even for generations.

of a few, very corrupt councillors, but there was a limit to the number he could select and to the time he could spend in such investigations. Paris was better organized, and in 1667 was given a better police force, but this was especially necessary because it was a natural centre for vagabonds and harboured all the principal intellectuals, both groups featuring prominently in any seditious movements which might arise from time to time.

If Colbert was not wholly successful in his reforms, he at least improved the efficiency of the administration, reduced the differences in outlook and policy between the localities and the central government and extended the control of the royal ministers over the kingdom. Much remained as it was, however, and even his improvements were not achieved rapidly. They occupied every minute of his twenty-two years as minister, and there was much he was not able to attempt. A major cause of his partial failure was his rivalry with Louvois, and Louis XIV deliberately played off the two ministers against each other. Louvois was gaining supreme influence in the last years of Colbert's life, and Louis favoured his glorious military plans, even though they undermined the economic health of France. To the king no price was too high to pay for a prestigious victory.

All provinces of France and all levels of society suffered, in addition to their other miseries, from the regular presence of the soldiery, who were renowned for their lawlessness and riotous behaviour. The seventeenth century had seen the slow development of a standing army, to defend the kingdom and to protect the king from the rebellious ambitions of his greater subjects. Although Louvois continually tried to impose high standards of training and discipline on the troops, the burden of billeting and of providing supplies was a grievous one for many provinces. The first war of the personal rule had been short, lasting from 1667 until 1668 and bringing substantial territorial gains in the east and north-east. From this moment Europe became alarmed, and coalitions built up against France. The 1672–8 Dutch War brought favourable peace terms, albeit after a prolonged and exhausting struggle, and the next ten peaceful years saw Louis as the unchallenged master on the European scene. However, from 1680 the glory of Louis XIV began slowly to dim.

The greatest single expression of that monarch's glory was his enormous and elaborate court. Yet the permanent move to Versailles, to a fitting shrine for the cult of the Sun King, took place in 1682 when the apogee of the reign had passed. Even when the court was

still itinerant, its splendour had become legendary. Learning and the
arts were lavishly patronized, and rigorous censorship prevented any
excessively outspoken criticism of the regime. All enterprises which
might increase the reputation of France were given the royal blessing.
The most important and potentially dangerous nobles were showered
with honorary offices and kept firmly within sight of the throne,
while a host of other aristocrats flocked to court in search of favour and
patronage. Some of these men chose to stay within easy distance of
the king and created a way of life for themselves out of what became
a boring round of complicated and expensive etiquette, made tolerable
only by the hope of catching a ministerial or royal eye. Others paid
more fleeting visits in search of honours, and then returned to the
provincial centres where they had estates, office and influence. Despite
the crowds of aristocrats in the garden at Versailles, the nobles were
still the powerful men in the provinces on whose co-operation royal
ministers had to rely if their policies were to be successful.

When war subsided temporarily in the 1680s Louis XIV, while
continuing to intimidate other, preferably smaller, European powers,
turned his attention to another of his obsessions, which was second
only to his quest for military glory – the imposition of religious uni-
formity throughout the realm. Although this had always been one
of his most cherished dreams, he pursued it more vigorously during
the late 1670s when a new wave of piety swept over him, stimulated
by his Jesuit confessor and by the last of his many mistresses, the only
one seriously to have influenced his policies, the devout Madame de
Maintenon. The atmosphere of Versailles was filled with this new religious fervour, a marked contrast with the more frivolous splendours of
the court as it travelled with the younger king. The religious problem
was threefold – there were still the Huguenots to eliminate, the trouble-
some Jansenists to curb and the claims of Rome to reject. Before the
end of the century there would also be the mystical Quietists to combat.

Richelieu and Mazarin had not liked the survival of a Huguenot
party in France, but the need for alliances with Protestant powers
abroad had tempered their desire to destroy it. Louis himself steadily
imposed further restrictions on the Huguenots by twisting the clauses
of the Edict of Nantes, and in 1679, with European peace assured and
armed with his new religious zeal, he increased the rate of persecution.
Moreover, Colbert was approaching his death and his influence was
waning, so that his pleas on behalf of the industrious Protestant craftsmen and merchants went unheeded. Despite the minister's objections

because of the loss of revenue, tax concessions were offered to converts from the heretic faith, while soldiers were cruelly billeted by Louvois on those who remained obdurate. In 1685 the Edict of Fontainebleau revoked the Edict of Nantes, and officially there were no longer any Protestants in France. Although the effects of the Revocation have been exaggerated, there is no doubt that the exodus of Huguenots from France did harm her economy, and enriched the talents of her competitors. In addition it aroused the hostility of many Protestant states and brought no compensating offers of friendship from Catholic rulers or from the Pope. Many Catholic Frenchmen applauded the Revocation itself, but condemned the cruelty with which it was implemented, while a large number of the Huguenots simply feigned conversion, thereby gaining exemption from taxes but remaining as a potentially subversive force within the kingdom.

Nor was the Jansenist problem finally solved in the 1680s. In the years before the Frondes, the Jansenists had acquired a number of adherents from the *noblesse de robe*, which increased the distrust felt for them by the royal ministers. Although many members of the sect condemned the parlementary Fronde, a number of important Frondeurs frequented their headquarters at Port-Royal, so that the government felt this group, with its rigorous and arid intellectual beliefs, to be a threat to the order of the state. In 1668, after lengthy disputes, the 'Peace of the Church' brought a temporary victory over the Jansenists who, it seemed, had acknowledged their theological errors. But Port-Royal remained a centre for important and pious visitors, and produced morally severe works which were widely circulated. In 1679 expulsions from Port-Royal were authorized, although the king had too many other preoccupations, particularly the Huguenots, to carry his policy to its conclusion. Another impediment was the antagonism between Louis and the Pope, which antedated the increased persecution of Jansenists and Huguenots. The Pope would have welcomed such an assault on heresy had not Louis offended Rome in 1673 by extending to the whole kingdom his right to receive the revenues of vacant sees. The militant Pope Innocent XI, who ascended the throne of St Peter in 1676, was not prepared to permit this initiative and in 1680 refused to accept some royal nominees for benefices. Although most of the French clergy, some with misgivings, loyally supported the Gallican position of the king, the Pope declined to give way, and it was only his death in 1689 which ended a position of stalemate.

From 1680 the monarchy slowly took a downward path and its opponents became more outspoken. There had been local revolts throughout the personal rule, but they were short-lived, and were prompted by specific taxes or attacks on privileges. Sometimes incited by local nobles, especially by the officials of the royal law courts, they differed little from the disturbances which frequently disrupted the reign of Louis XIII and the minority of Louis XIV himself. In the fifteen years after the Revocation more elaborate and sustained reform plans appeared, firstly from Huguenot writers and secondly from some of the aristocrats who gathered round the king's grandson, the Duc de Bourgogne, voicing a more general disquiet which many Frenchmen were feeling. The policies of the ministers did not seem to be bringing great benefits, and the old society and institutions which they were undermining seemed preferable. Not that these reformers were simply reactionaries. It is true that they were mostly aristocrats and did indeed seek to revive the role of the higher aristocracy as advisers of the crown, in place of those men of more recent origins who had failed to solve France's problems; but they also advocated some decentralization of power, which was not so unrealistic because local ties were strong, and men still felt a more real loyalty to their province than to the Paris government. Those provinces which were ruled for the king by aristo-cratic governors and administered by their local Estates seemed more efficient than the *pays d'élections*. The aristocrats could therefore quote much evidence in support of their beliefs and of their class, although none of them thought of limiting the royal power of decision. It was simply the advisers who needed to be changed, the familiar slogan of loyalty to the king but hatred of his ministers.

In fact the ministers like Colbert and Louvois were succeeded by inferior men from the same social background, and the financial situa-tion worsened. Nevertheless Colbert's son, the Marquis de Seignelay, did make an effective attempt at continuing his father's policies, despite the influence at court of Louvois. The great war minister himself died in 1691, leaving France to fight the long war of the League of Augsburg in which, from 1688 to 1697, most of Europe demonstrated its hostility to Louis XIV. The Treaty of Ryswick in 1697 contrasted sharply with the Nymegen Treaty of 1678, because the king had to concede where before he had gained. Moreover this was but a pause in the conflict. The knotty question of the succession to the Spanish throne when its childless king should die, which finally occurred in 1700, affected every European country. When Louis decided to champion the claims of his grandson Philippe, another war was precipitated, which lasted from 1702 until peace was eventually made at Utrecht in 1713.

The long financial crisis of the later reign was not simply caused by the cost of the wars. There was the disruption of trade, but above all this was a period of severe economic depression. Riots were frequent, not least among the Huguenots who still survived despite cruel persecution. Peasants died of starvation and groups of unruly beggars increased. There was a sharp contrast between the lower levels of society and those financiers who were prospering by exploiting the urgent financial needs of the government. Many men realized that reform of the finances and the tax system was vital, but that could be attempted only in a time of peace and relative prosperity. The crown would dearly have loved to buy back surplus offices which wasted precious revenue, but instead had to create more of them. One of the ablest ministers, Pontchartrain, tried every method of solving the crisis, even listening to some of the aristocratic reformers and trying their plans for a new tax which fell on all classes – though this was imposed simply as an emergency and therefore temporary levy, known as the Capitation in 1695 and the Tenth in 1710. These taxes suffered the same fate as others, the wealthy escaping from payment of their full share and the peasantry bearing the extra load which resulted. A single bad harvest was enough to make conditions intolerable.

Although the personal rule of Louis XIV had begun with poor harvests, especially that of 1662, the ten years before the Dutch War were almost free from such disasters and from the plagues which usually accompanied them. Prices were low, and industry and commerce prospered. The years 1674–84 were in contrast very hard, conditions improving in 1685–8, but then the situation deteriorated until real disaster struck in 1693–4, when a terrible harvest caused numerous deaths, perhaps a tenth of the whole population dying within a few months. Whatever this meant in human terms, to the government it meant the loss of vital taxpayers at a crucial moment. Although the financiers could profit by financing the war and thus compensate for the decline in revenue from their tax farms, the merchants also found the 1690s a decade of hardship. Trade had prospered during the 1680s, but during the War of the League of Augsburg the ports declined considerably, and industry was affected by the return of foreign craftsmen to their native lands.

A brief period of improvement followed the Ryswick Treaty of 1697. A few good harvests, a sudden increase in trade and reductions in taxation changed gloom to hope. But success still lay in the future, and the government needed stronger financial resources before it could reduce office-holding and abolish the temporary measures it had resorted to under pressure. Another great war ended such fantasies, and once again the crown used any means of raising money, however unfortunate. The finance ministers Chamillart and Desmarets simply could not solve the problem, and desperate remedies like the manipulation of the coinage greatly harmed the state's credit. In 1709 and 1710, when the war was going worse than ever, the climate again added its contribution to the worries of the ministers. At various times of the reign there had been reports of peasants living in caves and subsisting on roots, and in 1676 Locke had discovered Provençal peasants lunching on slices of congealed blood fried in oil, but the crisis of 1709 was far worse. Terrible reports reached Versailles of innumerable deaths from hunger, and even of cannibalism among starving children. If Louis saw an improvement in his military fortunes towards the end of the war, the harvests showed no inclination to follow suit, and 1715 found the country in the depths of poverty.

Tragedy rewarded the prayers of the king, his advisers and the aristocratic reformers that the next reign might see a turn for the better. The heir to the throne died in 1711, and in the following year the king's grandson, the Duc de Bourgogne, on whom the reformers had pinned their hopes, died within six days of his delightful wife, leaving a two-year-old as heir to his great-grandfather. Although there was barely a single Frenchman who could remember the days when Louis XIV had not ruled, the prospect of a long regency meant an opportunity for the ambitious to further their own careers, and the scheming began.

The one major attempt made by any French minister to reorganize the whole of the kingdom, that of Colbert, had been far from completely successful and had been virtually abandoned at his death. Many of the king's wisest advisers had died as well during the last fifteen years of the reign, and the old king was reluctant or unable to find adequate replacements. There was a dearth of talent for ruling France during the minority of Louis XV.

French Society in the Eighteenth Century

Eighteenth-century France witnessed an ever-increasing divergence in society, between the poor countryside with its depressed and backward peasantry and the rising, expanding populations of the towns whose leading citizens possessed great wealth. The peasants formed about four-fifths of the 20,000,000 Frenchmen alive in 1700. This figure remained quite constant, with temporary fluctuations, throughout the seventeenth and early eighteenth centuries, giving France a healthy lead over the populations of other European nations until they began to catch up rapidly in the eighteenth century. Although the French peasants were always poor, they recovered a little economic ground in the first few years of the Regency. Some good harvests, combined with the lessening pressure on land afforded by depopulation, compensated for the heavy burden of taxes and the reduction in the number of taxpayers. Still, there were plenty of taxpayers left, even if their ranks did not include the wealthiest fifth of the nation. The methods of agriculture and industry had not improved, but at least a large number of Frenchmen were at work again under peacetime conditions; the hinterlands of the ports were more prosperous, because overseas trade had been increasing steadily since just before 1700; the construction of more army barracks reduced the need for widespread billeting and made the presence of a nearby army a less terrifying fact. It is true that there were years of misery when some epidemic paid an irregular visit to a few provinces and carried off an extra large share of the inhabitants, but these crises never equalled those of 1693 and 1709. Although many small peasant proprietors lost their land and sought work as servants or as day labourers working for the increasing group of larger owners of land or industry, without which they had to join the roaming vagabonds, there was nevertheless a marginal improvement in the conditions of the humble townsman and peasant during the eighteenth century.

Not that this changed his suspicious attitude towards the government. Every new royal approach always seemed to herald an attack on local privileges or a novel tax. Change was always for the worse. Although the peasant had to pay the additional burden of seigneurial and ecclesiastical dues, it was those paid to distant and remote Paris which were most disliked and which, by their sheer magnitude, formed the really cruel burden upon him. If there were a few richer peasants in a village, they soon moved to the towns because they found that, if they stayed behind, they were required to pay an extra tax contribution in order that the sum demanded from the parish by the crown could be paid in full, despite the inability of some of their poorer neighbours to find the money for their own share. The localities continued to defend their still considerable rights with as much fervour as they had in the preceding century, more so perhaps as the attempts to undermine them became more regular. Such privileges frustrated the ministers of Louis XV and Louis XVI, just as they had in the personal rule of Louis XIV. The *intendant* remained the mouthpiece voicing the king's wishes throughout the countryside, but he was now listening more and more to local complaints and was often influenced by what he heard. An ever more busy man, he and his *sub-délégués* could do no more than tidy up the confused loose ends of provincial administration. Major reform was beyond their means and sometimes beyond their inclinations.

The provinces were administered as before, no matter how watchful the *intendant*, by the same profusion of officials, and by the tax-farmers who at least proved to be better at collecting taxes than the royal bureaucrats and made a profitable living for themselves at the same time. The familiar brakes on centralized power had largely survived – the local representative Estates or assemblies in Brittany, Languedoc, Burgundy and Provence, the *parlements* and other sovereign courts, the municipalities and the guilds. The crown never ceased to undermine these immunities and rights, but it ostentatiously respected them as long as they remained, knowing too well the tiresome disruption of provincial life which might follow from a disregard for them.

At the top of the social pyramid were the illustrious and privileged ranks of the nobility and higher clergy, although the composition of these groups had changed since 1600. Many wealthy bourgeois, investing in office and in land, had risen during the seventeenth century through the noble hierarchy until some of them were aristocrats of considerable prestige, and an increasing number of marriages between these more recently ennobled families and those of greater antiquity had welded them into a more unified class. The high clergy too drew its members almost exclusively from the aristocracy. After 1715 the nobility became particularly keen to defend their privileged and traditional aristocratic life, based on landed wealth, because a new figure of immense power was gaining access to their ranks – the financier. For these financiers, and for certain other bourgeois who were now becoming very rich, nobility of office or of the sword was still the ultimate social goal. The leading financiers, who built impressive town houses and country châteaux, often married their daughters into poor but distinguished aristocratic houses and purchased nobility for their sons. This élite, recently elevated from the middle classes, was received courteously by the king at Versailles, for these were the men on whom his policies depended. The old nobility hated to see this social outrage and sought to preserve the superiority of their order, voicing their grievances through the high *noblesse de robe* of the *parlements* who, throughout the century, became the spokesmen for the aristocracy and the defenders of their rights. In the second half of the eighteenth century they tried to exclude *parvenus* from their ranks by imposing strict regulations about the noble ancestry of applicants for high *robe* office, but the rules proved unenforceable and money remained a sufficient qualification for even the most important posts.

The alliance of *robe* and *épée* was a formidable one. It was still true that the officer of the sovereign court worked at his profession in a manner which the ancient noble, 'living nobly', did not, but many old aristocratic families now regarded the high *robe* as a desirable and profitable group to join. The senior *robins* enjoyed great prestige and were well placed in the social hierarchy; they frequented the most fashionable salons of Paris, contributed to the discussions there and acquired friends from distinguished houses; above all they were building their own families into veritable dynasties, not only by advantageous marriages, but by the inheritance of offices, by the purchase of further offices for relatives, by investment in land, and by placing their sons in the more traditional noble callings of army and Church, thereby widening their sphere of influence further. The families of the sword had no choice but to ally with these powerful defenders of their privileges.[1]

Defence was necessary primarily because of attempts by the central government to tap the wealth and reduce the independence of the aristocracy. Not until the years immediately preceding the Revolution was there any need to protect their order against attacks by other groups in society. The royal ministers knew that financial reform and solvency were virtually impossible while the nobility were exempt from direct taxation and had a stranglehold on the courts and provincial institutions. The people, on the other hand, did not resent these privileges, regarding them simply as unexceptionable legal rights enjoyed by their holders. They too considered the government to be the really serious threat, and the *parlements* encouraged them in this belief. To complicate the picture further, the nobles and clergy were themselves split, as was the Third Estate, by the line separating rich and

[1] It was also from the ranks of the *robe* that some of the royal ministers came, who were to scourge the class in which they had originated.

poor, some nobles, still denied the right to participate in retail trade and probably disinclined to do so, bearing more resemblance to peasants than to *grands seigneurs*.

One final privileged group, the urban patriciate whose members had not sought noble office but had remained in the world of business, sometimes made common cause with the nobility against the crown but had little in common with them. The great guilds of merchants and craftsmen had been given a new lease of life by Colbert, because it was they who had to supervise the new regulations for commerce and industry which he had promulgated, and they rose to an even higher position of influence in the eighteenth century as the fortunes of their members increased. In some important provincial centres, such as Bordeaux and Toulouse, the wealthy guilds allied with *robe* and with *épée*, holding among themselves all the offices of *parlement* and city, mixing in the same salons to which they also invited the principal tax farmers, and thus forming an unshakeable body of wealth, power and privilege. With so secure a position in their province, these men did not care if the nobles at court sneered at their society for being 'provincial' – it offered greater security and rewards than the precarious world of favouritism at Versailles.

The theory of aristocratic superiority remained, of course, even though the middle and upper classes were drawing somewhat closer together. But for all this increase in wealth, the society of France remained essentially static for much of the eighteenth century. Few went to the colonies. Few indeed changed their place of residence permanently, certainly not straying beyond the province which was the only large geographical unit they comprehended.

Louis XV

In 1715 the forces of discontent saw their chance. The aristocratic reformers and the *parlementaires* seized the opportunity to establish a monarchy which was counselled by its traditional advisers, although the two groups did not agree about the degree of pre-eminence that should be accorded to the peerage and to the *parlements*. The peers, that small number of most illustrious aristocratic families which included some of the reforming writers, but also contained powerful provincial governors, influential favourites and powerless reactionaries, was united by certain major grievances which all its members held against Louis XIV and his ministers. Firstly the king had given his illegitimate children precedence over them, with the consent of a reluctant *parlement* which now reversed its decision. Secondly they loathed the advisers on whom Louis had relied, because of their low social origins and because peers had always been royal counsellors by right of birth. The third complaint was voiced only by those who had never been favoured with an office which carried real civil or political authority – namely that the peerage had been deprived of all power, by which they really meant not just that the peers as a class were offered no important role in the running of the state such as they had the right to expect, but that, and this was more galling, certain individual peers did indeed wield extensive authority as governors, diplomats and high officials at court while others were kept in a position of complete impotence. Now was the moment for a reassertion of their status as an élite group, so that all of them might exercise this kind of sway. The reformers among the peers and nobles genuinely believed that an aristocratic conciliar system would pursue more enlightened courses, reversing destructive bourgeois policies like Colbertian mercantilism, but the motives of most nobles were more limited and selfish. While the enlightened few advocated the universal taxes which would have solved the government's problems, the majority clung tenaciously to their exemptions.

The peers, high aristocrats and *parlements* became the leading spokesmen during the first days of the Regency. Louis XIV had realized that his hated nephew, the Duc d'Orléans, would have to be Regent, but had placed his heir in the hands of his beloved natural sons and had prescribed the composition of the council with which Orléans would govern. The Regent found little difficulty in setting aside the king's will, relying as he could on the support firstly of the nobles, who detested the royal bastards and hoped that the power of the bureaucracy would be curbed; secondly the *parlements*, who sought to regain their lost influence; and thirdly the Jansenists and all who loathed Madame de Maintenon and the Jesuits. The *parlement* was given back its right to remonstrate before registering edicts, and it in return confirmed the full power of the Regent and excluded the bastards. Under the licentious leadership of Orléans, society abandoned the piety and moralizing which Madame de Maintenon had imposed on it. Now too the higher aristocracy was given its chance, as the Regent implemented some of the proposals of the reformers, notably by creating the series of councils known as the 'Polysynodie'. These noble bodies, composed of *robe* and *épée*, were inefficient and consequently short-lived, being suppressed in 1718, and the secretaries of state were left in sole charge of the central bureaucracy. The first noble reaction had failed and for the peers it was a permanent defeat. They had lost their opportunity of gaining a real position of pre-eminence, and their rivals as leaders of the nobility, the high *robe*, were to be the vocal champions of aristocracy from then on. The peers, by their arrogance, had alienated other members of the ancient nobility, who therefore welcomed the more reasonable counter-claims of the prestigious and respected members of the *parlement* of Paris. They, in all their elaborate panoply and ceremony, did not need to protest on behalf of the forces of reaction while Orléans was Regent, and rejoiced at their increased authority.

The principal task for the government was the reform of the crippled royal finances. If the Polysynodie was a failure, there had been a sufficient revival of noble influence to make inappropriate any talk of new taxes which all classes would pay. A *chambre de justice* was instituted to extract money from the financiers, but although it condemned many smaller ones, with scant regard for justice, the wealthy survived unscathed. The Regent pinned his hopes for financial reform on one man, the Scot John Law, whose great plans began to unfold in 1716. He acquired personal control of all tax collection, and tried to persuade everyone into trading with North America. Many speculators took the risk but the whole basis of the venture was unsound, and the scheme collapsed in 1720, leaving a few men with considerable fortunes but many more completely ruined. Although this stimulus to commerce did last, the disaster confirmed the already prejudiced views of the upper social levels that the world of trade and credit was dubious and unsafe.

In 1723 the Regent died, and the next senior prince of the blood, the Duc de Bourbon, took over the government until Fleury, the Bishop of Fréjus, engineered his downfall in 1726. Fleury then held office until 1743, so that once again a cardinal, which he became in 1726, had supreme ministerial power in France with the entire confidence of the king. After the long years of expensive war, Orléans' foreign minister, Dubois, and after that Fleury himself steered a peaceful but strong course in foreign affairs, so that one sizeable drain on revenues subsided and there was a chance for the royal finances to recover. The length of Fleury's ministry is remarkable because he was already seventy-three in 1726, and yet he was to create the most efficient team of ministers in the whole of eighteenth-century France, led by the great chancellor d'Aguesseau and containing some able secretaries of state. Despite all the skill of the cardinal as a master of diplomacy, pursuing peaceful policies, war could not for ever be avoided, but a short war from 1734 until 1736 led to a profitable peace with no real exhaustion for France. This long spell of calm on the international front gave the crown an opportunity to bring some order to its own affairs and into the country, in so far as this was ever possible.

One group of subjects whom Louis XIV had failed to bring to heel became a focal point for more general discontent in these early years of the new reign – the Jansenists. In 1713 the Bull *Unigenitus* marked the successful conclusion of lengthy negotiations between the king, strongly influenced by his Jesuit confessor, and Pope Clement XI. The bull, an attack on the writings of Pasquier Quesnel (1634–1719), was deliberately worded so as to avoid offending Gallicans, but bishops and *parlementaires* did not wholly approve of it and the *parlements* declined to register the edict enforcing its acceptance, demanding a number of modifications. When the Pope tried to insist on its observance by refusing to consecrate certain nominees for vacant sees, the *parlements* supported some bishops in protesting against it. The religious issue was of little concern to the sovereign courts, who were simply continuing their long fight to gain cognizance of all matters concerning ecclesiastical discipline, but whatever their reasons, these challengers of Rome were regarded sympathetically by the chief minister, Bourbon. When Fleury replaced him, policy changed. Fleury purged the episcopate of undesirables, and chose as bishops high aristocrats who were prepared to follow the lead of Versailles, which prompted the *parlements* to champion the lower clergy. Jansenism was becoming particularly dangerous because it was gaining a wider, popular appeal as a new miraculous element, totally foreign to the spirit of the founders of the movement, received superstitious acclaim from the lower classes. Although these manifestations of enthusiasm were controlled, the Jansenist dispute lasted into the middle years of the century.

Meanwhile the commercial revival of the last years of Louis XIV's reign was continuing. Colonial trade was increasing rapidly and in 1722 a *bureau de commerce* was created to assist overseas expansion. Prosperity came to Marseille, Dunkirk, Le Havre, La Rochelle, Nantes and above all to Bordeaux where merchants built themselves handsome houses and commissioned public buildings fitting for the centre of so great a city, and for the massive commercial transactions taking place within them. In other French towns beautiful schemes for rebuilding were devised, while Paris grew into new fashionable suburbs as well as reconstructing its centre.

Industry did not improve in the same way. For the first half of the century the regulations imposed during the ministry of Colbert were implemented quite rigidly, under the direction of the guilds and the royal officials who provided the link between them and the Paris government. But control and restriction tended to discourage innovations in method, and industry still relied on the labour of domestic workers using traditional means. In contrast to overseas trade, the internal commerce of France was still hampered by customs barriers, especially that between the *cinq grosses fermes* and the other provinces. Reform plans leading to a unified customs area were successfully opposed on many occasions by the principal tax farmers, and the dues which thus survived required a host of officials and collectors. There was an extensive scheme for building roads, but these routes corresponded more to the needs of the government than to those of commerce because they radiated from the capital. Not, of course, that the importance of good contacts between the central and provincial administrations should be decried, because one of the worst features of the French government was the time taken by Paris to communicate with its agents in the more distant regions of the kingdom. In Colbert's day, however, some commercial routes would have had higher priority.

Among the peasantry, little changed or improved. The population based on the land was now beginning to grow, and with it the number of vagabonds and bands of casual labourers. Poorly cultivated fields yielded increasingly meagre return for these rising numbers, and the poverty of the countryside began to contrast sharply with the wealth and therefore the attraction of the town.

Yet all was not peaceful in the France of Fleury. In 1737 he disgraced his foreign minister Chauvelin, who had been attempting to prosecute a more aggressive foreign policy and who had a faction of adherents behind him. Other factions were growing in Paris and at Versailles, and the secretaries of state themselves had united in opposition to the cardinal. Fleury's death in 1743 opened up new vistas for Chauvelin and other possible successors, but Louis XV followed his great-grandfather's example by refusing to replace Fleury with any comparably powerful minister. From then on he played off against each other ministers from the various factions who continued perpetually to intrigue at his court, where favourites and mistresses could hope to exercise stronger influence over the king than most of their predecessors had ever achieved over Louis XIV. For the secretaries of state, the refusal to appoint a first minister was a victory. But, whereas Louis XIV was a determined man who, having heard the advice of his secretaries, put forward his own decisive policies, Louis XV lacked confidence in his own powers of decision and failed to pursue consistent plans of action. More and more he preferred to hunt and to devote himself to his mistresses, and especially to the girl from a financier family who in 1745 became the official royal mistress with her title of Marquise de Pompadour. Now, under her supervision, the court began to be adorned in the best of taste, giving rise to complaints about extravagance and waste from the country. It is true that the sums spent were vast, but they were trifling compared to the cost of a full-scale war. The real financial problem had still not been faced – how to impose a universal tax to replace the existing revenues, which were derived from an inefficient system of farmed indirect taxes together with direct taxes which fell solely on the poorer elements in the state. Inadequate for running the administration and an expensive court, they would undoubtedly not permit a long period of war.

War, despite the efforts of Fleury, had begun before his death. The War of the Austrian Succession lasted from 1741 until 1748, and with it, from 1745 until 1754, came to power the controller-general of the finances, Machault d'Arnouville. Too often in the earlier years of the reign, the pressure from influential financiers had prevented a finance minister from gaining supremacy. The needs of war, which Machault managed to meet, gave him the opportunity for this kind of superiority and in 1749 he introduced a new direct tax, the Twentieth, to be levied on everybody, in the manner of the short-lived taxes of 1695 and 1710. Immediately the privileged classes took up an attacking position – the perpetual quarrel between centralized government and local liberties was as alive as ever. Involved in it were other disputes which had not been solved earlier in the century, notably that between Jansenists and Jesuits.

The *parlements* had not been completely docile since they regained their right to remonstrate before registering edicts in 1715. Although the provincial *parlements* usually gave way after repeated requests by the government, it was often only a personal appearance by the king which compelled the Paris *parlement* to obey the royal will. In 1717 it obtained the suppression of the new and hated tax on all classes, the Tenth. It tried unsuccessfully to oppose John Law more than once, and was exiled from Paris until after his fall and until it had moderated its opposition to the anti-Jansenist policies of the crown. It upset further plans for a small direct tax in 1725 and became deeply involved in the religious issue again in the 1730s, when it gained some ground for the Gallican and Jansenist side at the cost of the exile of certain *parlementaires*. Between 1733 and 1748 its role was more peaceful, though it still made efforts to limit the temporary imposition of new direct taxes, and this relative calm was brought about largely by the care of the ministers in not raising issues which might provoke it to react. Thus the *parlements* were by now clearly to be seen as the principal defenders of fiscal and provincial liberties, and of Gallican and Jansenist beliefs against the policies of ultramontanes like Fleury and the Jesuits, although in foreign affairs they offered no opinion. Similarly the king made it plain that he was not prepared to share one jot of his authority with them. The *parlements* still based their claims on the fact that they were defending French traditions against the evil acts of the royal ministers, and in addition, of course, they continued to carry out their extensive tasks in their capacity as the principal law courts of the realm. It was unfortunate that in this period of their great and increasing influence there was a decline in the general standard of professionalism among their members, with a few notable exceptions.

The opposition shown by the *parlements* to John Law and the new taxes began to gain them regular and reliable popular support, which they had not enjoyed in the past for any length of time, and their Gallican views brought them the staunch backing of the lower clergy as well. By 1748 the central government realized that the *parlements* could cause a general uprising if they were alienated, a threat as serious as the government's own ability to imprison or exile members of or even whole *parlements*. These sovereign courts were quick to sense any plot to erode privileges and change the almost mythical constitution and fundamental laws of France, the *intendant* being the royal official whom they most readily suspected of complicity in such scheming. Many ordinary subjects shared the *parlementaire* view that the king would act in his subjects' best interests if he were properly counselled, while theorists still distinguished between 'absolute' and 'arbitrary' monarchy, between monarchy and tyranny. If these were misguided beliefs, it was at least true that the decisions taken in Paris bore little resemblance to what was done by royal agents in the localities, and to what was desired by the people.

From the death of Fleury, whose influence had been waning since

1740, there was no supreme minister either to govern France or to become a focus for hatred. There were the Pompadour, the foreign minister d'Argenson and the controller-general Machault. With Machault's Twentieth of 1749, battle commenced. The *parlements* and the Estates had to be forced to register the edict instituting it; the nobles refused to pay and no tax-collector had the power to compel them to change their minds; and the clergy made the most vocal protests, supported by the Jesuits, by members of the royal family and by Machault's now powerless enemy, d'Argenson. Behind the controller-general was the full strength of the Pompadour. In 1751 the tax was suspended on clerical property, and Machault acknowledged that the finances could not be reformed in any drastic way.

Linked with this was a religious struggle. Although there were still conflicts between the crown and the Huguenots during the middle years of the eighteenth century, the crucial issue was now Jansenism. If the number of Jansenist bishops had declined under the Regency, the movement had continued to gain adherents among the lower clergy. Fleury had controlled the most extreme manifestations of their beliefs, but in 1750 a new outburst of fervour coincided with the disputes about the Twentieth. The upper clergy feared for their authority as the *curés*, supported by the *parlements*, claimed for the laity a greater share in the running of the Church. The king, influenced by the *dévots* at court, sided with the high clerics, even though this entailed the abandonment of Machault's financial proposals.

In 1753 the *parlement* of Paris strongly reasserted its right to defend the fundamental laws, assigning to itself as much authority as it dared without being plainly revolutionary. When Louis XV refused to receive these remonstrances, the *parlement* staged a judicial strike, and was promptly ordered into exile from the capital. When the legal profession refused to attend the new court which the king substituted for the *parlement*, compromise became unavoidable, and in 1745 the *parlementaires* returned to Paris in victorious mood. By this time, Jansenism was again receding from the scene, although the hostility of the lower clergy towards their superiors, and of the *parlements* towards the Jesuits, had not abated. If the king's affection for the Society of Jesus remained, he could no longer offer its members adequate protection.

Machault ceased to administer the finances in 1754 and two years later became chancellor, but, after further attempts to humiliate the *parlement* of Paris, he was disgraced in 1757. The king needed the support of the *parlementaires* in approving emergency measures for raising money to finance the Seven Years War, which began in 1756 and started badly for France, the situation improving only when Choiseul became foreign minister in 1758. Even so, the Peace of Paris, which ended the war in 1763, marked the virtual end of the French colonial empire. Thus in the difficult circumstances of war, a period of parlementary dominance began, and one in which the provincial courts drew closer and closer to their *confrères* in the capital. One merit of the parlementary case was that, although such steadfast opposition to fiscal innovation was not likely to solve the difficulties of the crown, it was at least consistent and was supported by sound legal precedent. The government, in contrast, continually resorted to hasty expedient and, when the opposing side gained too much ground, policies, revenues and ministers were sacrificed by the king as an offering to peace, co-operation and compromise. This was an age when royal advisers came and went with alarming rapidity, and factions rose and fell.

The Seven Years War over, the magistrates drastically curtailed plans to prolong new wartime taxes. At the same time they launched a further attack on the Jesuits, which led to the suppression of the Order in France by a reluctant Louis in November 1764. Disputes about the role of the *parlements* continued for the rest of the 1760s, and the king openly clashed with those of Paris and Brittany. By January 1771 they had created a state of near anarchy in the kingdom, and the crown could barely be said to be in control. Towards the end of that month, dramatic, swift and decisive action was taken – the chancellor Maupeou abolished the *parlement* of Paris!

Meanwhile Choiseul was trying to improve the quality of the armed forces, reducing the power of the greater officers and rebuilding the navy which the war had shown to be so vital. Yet his days of power were numbered, and once again, though for different reasons, the *parlement* of Paris and a royal mistress were involved. Choiseul had survived the death of his staunch advocate, Pompadour, in 1766, who had greatly influenced the fortunes of many individuals at court, and he had avoided becoming a victim of the customary parlementary hostility towards ministers because he gave way to the *parlements* whenever it was possible. They were not as upset by the loss of a colonial empire as they would have been by a new tax. Yet, although he successfully negotiated the marriage of the daughter of Empress Maria-Theresa, Marie-Antoinette, to the Dauphin in 1770, the king himself decided to disgrace him for showing considerable dislike for the new royal mistress, Madame du Barry, and for his subservience to the *parlements*, together with the evidence against him which had been collected by the anti-*parlementaire* Maupeou and controller-general Terray. In December 1770 Choiseul was stripped of all his powers and exiled, taking with him the support of the nobility, the sovereign courts and the general public, who designated the new mistress as the source of such intrigues. One positive result for France, however, was that this action averted the war which Choiseul had been planning.

The abolition of the *parlement* of Paris in the first month of the new year was a bold step, and was greeted with an outburst of protest from all privileged groups in society who had come to regard the courts as their defenders, even though differences remained between them. The king was thus shown to be in control after all, and men might well speculate as to where his power in fact ended. New courts were set up to fulfil the judicial role of the *parlement*, while opposition to the formulation of royal policy now ceased – though the problem of how these policies were to be implemented throughout the provinces was still very real.

At last Terray was able to propose financial reforms, unhampered by remonstrances. The long-cherished plans for a tax on all classes could be imposed. All that was needed was time – and with the sudden death of Louis XV in 1774, time began to run out.

Louis XVI

Under Maupeou and Terray it seemed that the monarchy had never been stronger, although it had seldom been less popular. The enlightened thinkers, who disliked the *parlements*, also opposed what they considered to be the unenlightened policies of these ministers, while the privileged orders loathed them for their dangerous radical nature. Not that the financial measures of Terray brought a great improvement in efficiency, and when Turgot took control of the finances in 1774 the crown was heavily overspending. Yet an annual deficit in 1774 of 37,000,000 *livres* was to rise to 112,000,000 by 1787, growing partly as a result of the cost of the heavy and itself ever-increasing public debt. War was the largest consumer of funds, and no financial expedient gave the monarch the means to meet these demands adequately. The king simply had to rely more and more heavily on the financiers, ironic in a country which was not denied some degree of prosperity in its commerce and industry. If ministers still dreamed, as Colbert had once done, of abolishing internal customs dues, the consequent loss of revenue ensured that such plans remained in the world of fantasy. Moreover there were limits beyond which one could not tax the peasantry – they had nothing further with which to pay. Turgot observed that the number of landless peasants and vagabonds was growing too, in a France which was considerably more densely populated than it had been fifty years before. Wealth was becoming more and more concentrated in fewer and fewer privileged hands.

Yet French society was fairly docile. There were spasmodic and localized disturbances in countryside and town, but no signs of grievances which might lead men to expect a revolution. It was higher in the social scale, among the upper bourgeoisie, that enlightened ideas were being discussed and resentment against the privileged orders was growing, but even here the concern was largely with the possible solution of practical problems, not with the underlying philosophical spirit.

The new king, grandson of Louis XV, did not receive equally wise counsel from all the ministers he chose to help him in his early years as king. Choiseul's hopes to reassert his influence were dashed by his enemies of the *dévot* party at court, who persuaded Louis XVI to look elsewhere, and Maurepas, a capricious intriguer, became his chief adviser. The unpopular ministers of his grandfather's last years were not long to survive and new names appeared – Vergennes in foreign affairs, Miromesnil as chancellor, and of course Turgot as controller-general of finances. With Turgot, who had already carried into effect a number of reforms as *intendant* of Limoges, the philosophers believed that a minister after their own heart had at last come to power. Turgot believed in complete freedom for commerce and industry, and in basing taxation not on those sectors of the economy but on landed wealth. However he realized that caution and gradual change were the only methods at his disposal. Although no lover of the *parlements*, he did feel it wise to restore the magistrates to a part of their former authority, in the hope of gaining some support for the new government and of avoiding further *dévot* influence. He confidently believed that his plans for enlightened reform would have sufficient appeal that the courts would never again have such widespread support from the country. He began, not by following Maupeou's method of attacking strong institutions, but by introducing moderate financial reforms during 1774 and 1775. One of them was the abolition of the practice by which the wealthier members of parishes had to pay the taxes which their poorer fellows had failed to produce, while innovations in 1776 included a tax on landowners to pay for road building and maintenance, which had formerly been carried out by conscripting free labour from the local peasantry. Another edict abolished most of the Paris guilds. These decrees were forced through an unwilling *parlement* and the peasantry rejoiced, but the complaints of the privileged orders prompted Maurepas to engineer the dismissal of Turgot. His successor, Clugny, quickly undid his work during a few brief months in office, and the king now began to consider an expensive war policy which Turgot had always rejected.

France was to be involved in the War of American Independence from 1778 until 1783 under the guidance of Vergennes, one of the longest-serving ministers of the reign, who steered foreign policy from 1774 until his death in 1787. To provide the necessary funds, the Swiss financier Necker was appointed as director of the state's finances and, although he believed in a partially restrictive commercial policy, basically continued Turgot's programme of piecemeal financial reform. He also kept the support of the privileged orders for some time, but he was never liked by Maurepas who became keener to replace him as the months went by. By 1781 the magistrates too were objecting, their grievance being his partly implemented scheme for setting up new provincial assemblies. Maurepas seized this chance to force Necker to resign but himself died before the year was out, leaving Vergennes as chief minister though without such supreme authority. The next two controllers-general, Joly de Fleury and d'Ormesson, soon provoked opposition and were removed, leaving the office vacant for Calonne.

Calonne spent lavishly on public works to restore confidence in the government, but began to plan reforms, especially a novel universal tax which was to be administered by new local assemblies, composed of men from all the social orders. Resorting to a device which had not been employed since the ministry of Richelieu, he suggested that the king should invite carefully selected men to an Assembly of Notables, in order that these plainly revolutionary proposals might be supported by this sample of the privileged orders, making it more difficult for the magistrature to stage a wholehearted attack on them. As Calonne had rejected piecemeal reform in favour of more massive changes, it was only through an Assembly of Notables or the Estates-General that he could hope to persuade the country to accept such innovations from the government. He considered the latter institution to be cumbersome and antiquated and that it would not serve his purpose, but, as it turned out, the Notables were far from amenable. Their hostility was vented upon the plans from the opening of the assembly in February 1787, and in April he was dismissed. His successor, Loménie de Brienne, was a stern critic of his policies and was accordingly more acceptable to the Notables, who became more co-operative. Yet the outcome was not a royal victory, for, against a background of numerous pamphlets, the Notables recommended and soon the *parlement* demanded the summoning of the Estates-General, as being the only body competent to discuss such matters. Judicial, clerical and public opinion joined in the clamour that it should assemble at once. Under Turgot, Necker and Calonne, hope of enlightened reform had begun to appear more feasible and an improvement seemed in sight, even if privilege always remained a barrier. Now privilege had triumphed.

The interminable disputes between the privileged orders and the royal ministers were not the only cause of contention during the last decades of the *ancien régime*. At the peak of the social pyramid there was the controversial figure of Marie-Antoinette, living her pleasurable life where the people of France never glimpsed her, and always suspect because of her Austrian birth. In fact she had tried hard to forget her fatherland and become truly French, but pamphleteers attributed every kind of scandalous behaviour to her and she was accused of many an intrigue. In 1785 the affair of the diamond necklace finally dragged her name through the worst kind of social mire.

The court nobility who plotted against ministers did not represent the interests of all nobles. The provincial aristocracy, whom the great courtiers ridiculed for their rusticity, disliked the court nobles as much as they hated the ministers, and were more concerned to revive the power of local assemblies and courts than to support the *parlement* of Paris. Further tension was growing in the provinces because, although some nobles were keen to farm their estates efficiently or participate in new industrial developments, many preferred to boost their income by exploiting their feudal dues and rights to the limit. Yet the peasantry reacted by opposing specific instances of such exploitation, still not condemning the whole concept of privilege.

Townsmen were in their perpetual state of ambivalence, castigating noble exemptions but keen to acquire nobility themselves. Equally they disliked the despotic aims of the crown, and it was difficult to do that without supporting the champions of privilege. Moreover there was a gulf as wide as ever between humble townsman and great bourgeois, and between peasant and lord, and between lowly *curé* and prince of the Church. Clerical taxation seemed to go into the pockets of remote ecclesiastical nobles, and was accordingly hated by the taxpayers, although once again the assault was on the specific burden, not the whole principle.

The eventful reign of Louis XVI took place against this general backcloth of discontent and poverty. Increased population led to high prices and a shortage of grain, which might be satisfactory for the peasant with produce to sell, but not for the labourer, the peasant who was not fully self-supporting, or the poorer townsman who had to pay the prices. Landowners were changing from arable to pasture, and the resulting unemployed joined the rootless men who swamped the small towns, for whom adequate poor relief could not be provided. No government could afford to give the necessary substantial aid, although an *intendant* could assist a little on occasions by some form of tax relief. Turgot tried to help the needy more effectively, but lack of funds curtailed his success and later ministers showed less willingness to continue his policy.

The poor at times were pushed to the point of revolt. A short but severe food crisis in 1775 prompted grain riots in Paris and the neighbouring provinces, aimed specifically against Turgot's policy of free trade in grain. The bourgeoisie, who stood to gain from this free trading and who approved of this enlightened minister, opposed these revolts while army and clergy helped the crown to suppress them. A rebellion by the lower orders alone could not hope to succeed. There were further spasmodic local riots between 1775 and 1786, and towards the end of this period there were disturbances in Paris in which the tax-farmers and the Church were the targets. These hostilities were still the work of disunited social groups, acting individually against the government and other tax-collecting bodies. Even at this late date they did not feel that their principal grievances could be blamed on whole classes in society.

In 1787 the political atmosphere began to undergo drastic change. The Paris *parlement* accepted the newly created provincial assemblies, but opposed innovations in taxation and was exiled. Strong protests from the other sovereign courts caused its reinstatement, and its return was signalled not only by popular acclaim but also by rioting among the clerks of the lower courts and among journeymen and apprentices in the luxury industries. The *parlement* loudly supported the clamouring for the Estates-General and the people of Paris were delighted, not yet being aware that their champions, although containing a group of reformers, were in reality the strongest bastion of privilege.[1] A further royal attack on the stubborn *parlementaires* in 1788 provoked such a violent outcry in the provinces, chiefly in those with *parlements* and those which still possessed, or had formerly possessed, Estates of their own, that again it was allowed to return to the capital, this time more triumphantly than ever, in September. The minister responsible was once more Necker, who had replaced Brienne in August. Then the *parlement* declared its true hand. Insisting that voting in the forthcoming Estates-General be based on the equal influence of each individual Estate, and opposing the Third Estate's demand for double representation, thereby ensuring that the privileged classes could always outvote the Third, they revealed their championship for the old order and much of their support vanished. The Third Estate now saw an enemy where a friend had stood.

Meanwhile, in the provinces, the new assemblies aroused the opposition of the nobility and clergy, who in the *pays d'états* petitioned the weak government successfully for the summoning of their old Estates, which met at various dates during 1787 and 1788. This aristocratic initiative was supported by riots of lawyers' clerks, aided by humble townsmen and peasants who had come to the towns, and directed against the increasingly impotent *intendant*, but the greater bourgeois were becoming unhappy with this leading role which the privileged accorded themselves. It was the process of electing deputies in early 1789 to the Estates-General which would really expose these differences. Thus in the winter of 1788-9 the crown could not rely on its officials, and it often dared not actively support the *intendant*, but at least it could take heart that the battlefield had shifted and now lay between the Third Estate and the privileged orders. In the elections of deputies it was not simply that the Third Estate rejected the leadership of the nobility. The provincial aristocrats rejected that of the high court nobles as well, and the composition of the Second Estate reflected this divergence. The upper clergy were less reactionary, but many higher churchmen deemed it wiser to join with the privileged orders, and the more lowly *curés* made common cause with the Third Estate so

---

[1] Although these reformers were to play a significant role in later years and were very different from the rest of the *parlementaires*, they shared their more reactionary colleagues' hearty disapproval of the ministers and their arbitrary methods. Therefore it suited them to agree to a united parlementary attack on the central government.

that it was their deputies who dominated their order when the assembly met.

Faced with the aggressive stance of the nobility, the government of Necker, harassed on all sides and in an impossible situation, decided to support the Third Estate in its demand for double representation and was suddenly popular in the towns again. If the privileged were to be defeated, the crown was to be the leader of the attacking forces. On 31 December 1788 the conflict was still basically between town and country. The peasantry, in despair after the two brutal harvests of 1787 and 1788, were not yet making a violent onslaught on their *seigneurs*, even though they might be hoping that the Estates-General would produce some improvement in their position. The more outspoken views of the Third Estate were those of townsmen, who had greater cause to loathe the nobility.

For all the tensions within it, French society had remained unchanged in all its essentials for the two hundred years before 1787. In two years a wholly new climate developed, grievances were being formulated in novel terms, and new ideas were emerging from drawing-room discussions and beginning to catch hold of men's minds throughout the country.

Bibliography

French historians and their publishers have a masterly knack of producing intro-ductory books which are both concise and profound, outlining a subject clearly and at the same time summarizing the latest researches associated with it. The new student of early modern French history can therefore have no better guide than the slim volumes by Hubert Méthivier in the 'Que sais-je?' series: *L'Ancien Régime* (Paris, 1961); *Le Siècle de Louis XIII* (Paris, 1964); *Le Siècle de Louis XIV*, 2nd ed. (Paris, 1960); and *Le Siècle de Louis XV* (Paris, 1966) (numbered 925, 1138, 426 and 1229 respectively in the 'Que sais-je?' catalogue). A book which covers the same ground as M. Méthivier, but in more detail, is R. Mandrou, *La France aux XVIIe et XVIIIe siècles* (Paris, 1970), in another celebrated series, the 'Nouvelle Clio', and like its companion volumes discusses the state of each topic, describes research at present in progress and considers the lacunae which remain to be filled. He is particularly strong on the recent economic and demographic studies whose varied and complex conclusions are here reduced to manageable proportions. A similar blend of overall structure, recent scholarship and unsolved problems is produced by J. Ellul, *Histoire des institutions de l'époque franque à la révolution*, 5 vols (Paris, 1969–72). A more dramatic presentation of this kind, less thorough and satisfying than M. Mandrou but directing vivid shafts of light on to the social scene in eighteenth-century France, is the anthology of extracts from other historians collected and introduced at length by Pierre Goubert in *L'Ancien*

Régime, Vol. I (Paris, 1969), now translated into English. Also in English is a contribution to the *New Cambridge Modern History*, Vol. VI, by one of the most distinguished historians of our time, Jean Meuvret, on 'The Condition of France 1688–1715'.

In recent years an English school of French historians has come into considerable prominence, some of whose members have written introductory works as well as volumes of penetrating scholarship. From the former category a number can be selected whose authors really understand the atmosphere and preoccupations of *ancien régime* society. C. B. A. Behrens, *The Ancien Régime* (London, 1967), is an admirable guide to the period 1748–89; J. H. Shennan, in the introductory chapter to his collection of documents *Government and Society in France, 1461–1661*, presents a clear but brief survey of the presuppositions underlying ideas of sovereignty, government and society in the seventeenth century and before; J. S. Bromley in his chapter on 'The decline of absolute monarchy 1683–1774' from the volume edited by J. M. Wallace-Hadrill and J. McManners, *France: Government and Society*, 2nd ed. (London, 1970), evokes the social climate of eighteenth-century France with as much brilliance as the author of the preceding chapter shows ineptitude in understanding the age of Louis XIV; the contribution to the same collection by Professor McManners – 'The Revolution and its antecedents 1774–94' – is also valuable, but so indeed is everything which he has written on the *ancien régime* and its fall.

In turning to more substantial works on French society, it is therefore most appropriate to begin with J. McManners, *French Ecclesiastical Society under the Ancien Régime: a Study of Angers in the Eighteenth Century* (Manchester, 1960), because he is able to bring to life with great clarity an area of provincial France at a crucial period of French social history. This book is not only penetrating and informative but is also a delight to read. The only other work of this quality in English is Olwen Hufton, *Bayeux in the Late Eighteenth Century: a Social Study* (Oxford, 1967). In French the recent social, economic and demographic studies have tended to become more and more restricted in their geographical and chronological scope, and increasingly technical in their concepts and language. In an essay of this kind, it is wise to recommend only a selection of the very best. Outstanding are the article by J. Meuvret, 'Les Crises de subsistances et la démographie de la France d'ancien régime', *Population* (1947); and the weighty books of E. Le Roy-Ladurie, *Les Paysans du Languedoc* (Paris, 1966); Pierre Goubert, *Beauvais et le Beauvaisis de 1600 à 1730, contribution à l'histoire sociale de la France au XVIIe siècle* (Paris, 1960); Marc Venard, *Bourgeois et paysans au XVIIe siècle: recherches sur le rôle des bourgeois parisiens dans la vie agricole au sud de Paris au XVIIe siècle* (Paris, 1957); Jean Meyer, *La Noblesse bretonne au XVIIIe siècle* (Paris, 1966); and Gaston Roupnel, *La Ville et la campagne au XVIIe siècle: étude sur les populations du pays dijonnais*, 2nd ed. (Paris, 1955). This last work first appeared in 1922, when it was not recognized as the masterpiece of rural history which it is now considered to be.

Turning now to more specific historical situations and themes, the reader finds that the ground is covered very unevenly and that, because the preoccupations of historians have shifted strongly in recent years towards the realm of social history, there are few books printed before 1955 which are still relevant to current historical debates. A notable exception is the now classic work of C. W. Cole,

Colbert and a Century of French Mercantilism, 2 vols (New York, 1939), and happily reprinted in 1964, which devotes substantial chapters to the economic policies of each seventeenth-century minister before commencing its valuable and nearly exhaustive analysis of the attempts made by Colbert to revive and expand all aspects of French economic life. A later volume by the same author, *French Mercantilism 1683–1700* (New York, 1943), takes the story through the more difficult years of the personal rule of Louis XIV.

The ministry of Richelieu has unfortunately given occasion for a number of disappointing or biased books, whose omission here is intended to discourage their perusal. Of noticeably higher quality and especial interest is a work from one of the small group of distinguished historians of France who come from the Soviet Union, Mme A. Lublinskaya, *French Absolutism: the Crucial Phase 1620–9* (Cambridge, 1968). After a few paragraphs to placate the Russian censor, of which the Western reader need take little note, she embarks firstly on an analysis of the current historiographical controversy about the possibility of a 'general crisis' in the seventeenth century, after which she examines the changing social situation during a vital decade of the ministry of Richelieu when, she convincingly argues, the balance of social forces moved and there was a significant development in the confrontation between the crown and its opponents from the privileged ranks of society.

The middle years of the seventeenth century, on which any supposed 'general crisis' is centred, have produced a flood of conflicting books and pamphlets, ranging from wild polemic to meticulous archival scholarship. The possible ways in which the situation in France can be related to or distinguished from more general European trends are most conveniently found in the single volume containing reprints of the articles which began the whole debate, and edited now by T. Aston, *Crisis in Europe 1560–1660: Essays from 'Past and Present' 1952–62* (London, 1965). Further controversy centres around the nature of the revolutionary movements in France itself at this period, springing originally from the work of another Russian historian, Boris Porchnev, *Les Soulèvements populaires en France de 1623 à 1648*, first published in Russian in 1948, appearing in French in a Paris edition of 1963. This thesis was soundly criticized in a lengthy review article by Roland Mousnier, 'Recherches sur les soulèvements populaires en France avant la Fronde', *Revue d'histoire moderne et contemporaine* (1958), which M. Porchnev answered in the French edition of his book. Too many other writers have since joined the battle to be listed here. Other aspects of the civil disturbances which disrupted France in the ministry of Mazarin have also given rise to prolonged argument. Among the most stimulating are P. R. Doolin, *The Fronde* (Cambridge Mass., 1935); E. H. Kossman, *La Fronde* (Leyden, 1954); A. Lloyd Moote, *The Revolt of the Judges: the Parlement of Paris and the Fronde 1643–52* (Princeton, 1971); and an article by Professor Moote, 'The Parlementary Fronde and Seventeenth-Century Robe Solidarity', *French Historical Studies*, II (1962).

The personal rule of Louis XIV has been less well served by recent historical scholarship. Too many historians have concentrated on the attempts to develop the central government machinery without adequately considering the way in which the royal administration worked in the localities. Yet, although it does not escape that particular criticism, Pierre Goubert, *Louis XIV et vingt millions de français* (Paris, 1966), translated as *Louis XIV and Twenty Million Frenchmen*

(London, 1970), provides one of the best surveys of many aspects of the reign. In the collection edited by J. Rule, *Louis XIV and the Craft of Kingship* (Ohio, 1969), there is a useful introduction by the editor, another thought-provoking piece from Professor Moote on the bureaucracy, a brilliant and densely packed contribution to the debate about the motivation of the king's foreign policy by Professor R. M. Hatton, and a reprint of the excellent article by H. G. Judge, 'Church and State under Louis XIV', originally published in *History*, XLV (1960). Unfortunately many of the remaining contributors to Professor Rule's volume fall well below this high standard. Perhaps the most important religious issue during the personal rule was the persecution and expulsion of the Huguenots, which is discussed by W. C. Scoville, *The Persecution of Huguenots and French Economic Development 1685–1720* (Berkeley/Los Angeles, 1960), who wisely modifies some of the more extreme generalizations which were previously current. Most other aspects of the declining years of the *roi soleil* still await their modern historians.

The same is true of the reign of Louis XV, although certain themes have been selected for recent study. The most significant single trend in eighteenth-century society was the *rapprochement* of the *noblesse d'épée* and the *noblesse de robe*, which is admirably discussed by F. L. Ford, *Robe and Sword: the Regrouping of the French Aristocracy after Louis XIV* (Cambridge Mass., 1953), although he makes some unwarranted assumptions about society in the preceding century. The whole question of a suggested aristocratic reaction in the last decades of the *ancien régime* has recently been examined and disputed more hotly, and the various positions have been clearly delineated and assessed by William Doyle, 'Was there an aristocratic reaction in pre-Revolutionary France?', *Past and Present*, LVII (1972). This eighteenth-century topic cannot be considered without reference to the preceding period, on which a significant light has been thrown by R. B. Grassby, 'Social Status and Commercial Enterprise under Louis XIV', *Economic History Review*, 2nd series, XIII (1960–1). On the aristocracy under Louis XV and Louis XVI there is the work of R. Forster, *The Nobility of Toulouse in the Eighteenth Century* (Baltimore, 1960); the chapter by J. McManners, 'France', in the collection edited by A. Goodwin, *The European Nobility in the Eighteenth Century* (London, 1953); the article by C. B. A. Behrens, 'Nobles, Privileges and Taxes in France at the End of the Ancien Régime', *Economic History Review*, 2nd series, XV (1962–3); and the more recent book by J. Egret, *Louis XV et l'opposition parlementaire 1715–74* (Paris, 1970).

The historians of the Revolution itself – although that topic is outside the scope of this essay – have obviously posited ideas about the *ancien régime* in their introductory pages. Some have shown little understanding of its methods of working, tensions, strengths and weaknesses, but there are a number who have truly comprehended its nature. Perhaps the most masterly work is Alfred Cobban, *The Social Interpretation of the French Revolution* (Cambridge, 1964), whose pages contain the mature reflections of a distinguished historian who had examined and re-examined these issues over the years. A great teacher, it is not surprising therefore that the volume of essays in memory of his life and work should contain fascinating contributions by pupils whose own scholarship is now renowned. J. F. Bosher has edited this tribute, *French Government and Society 1500–1850: Essays in Memory of Alfred Cobban* (London, 1973).

With a companion volume in this series on French thought, it seems improper here to attempt a summary of the vast literature on political and philosophical ideas, at times so intimately bound up with social and political problems during the *ancien régime*. Finally, then, a work of reference must be listed: Marcel Marion, *Dictionnaire des institutions de la France aux XVIIe et XVIIIe siècles* (Paris, 1923; reprinted 1968), which, though biased at times in its historical interpretations, is largely correct in its factual information and is an indispensable guide to the complex institutional terminology and regional variations of *ancien régime* administration.

FRENCH HISTORY AND SOCIETY
FROM THE REVOLUTION
TO THE FIFTH REPUBLIC

Douglas Johnson

The Revolution

Fortunate the historian who knows the starting-point of his subject. The French Revolution has been given various *points de départ*. Napoleon believed that it began with the affair of the queen's necklace (in 1785 the Cardinal de Rohan was arrested for having used the queen's name in order to procure a necklace without paying for it, a scandal which associated the queen's name with an unfortunate collection of crooks and intriguers). Others have suggested that French intervention in the War of American Independence, especially from 1780 onwards, was the principal cause of the French Government's amassing debts, and therefore perhaps represents most directly the beginning of the crisis. Certain modern historians tend to see the measures taken by the Government to meet the financial difficulties as creating the real conflict: thus Calonne, in August 1786, presented the king with important plans for the restoration of solvency and in February 1787 unsuccessfully confronted a special Assembly of Notables with his projects; Brienne, who succeeded Calonne, found himself in conflict with the *parlements*, and his attempt to create new assemblies led to aristocratic revolt in the provinces and to distinct signs of a breakdown of the Government's authority. These modern historians are joined by many contemporary observers in believing that the decision to summon the Estates-General (which had not met since 1614), the process of its election and its meeting on 5 May 1789, constituted a revolutionary situation. For everyone, the famous events of 14 July 1789 must be seen as the symptom of a long crisis, and not as its beginning.

But the difficulties of interpreting the beginning of the Revolution are not simply a matter of dates. For many historians the collapse of the *ancien régime* was a simple enough matter. They saw a system of government which had become impossible. Not only was it oppressive and corrupt, it was also overwhelmed by a variety of crises which it could not resolve. And traditionally, the greatest of these crises was a class struggle. A privileged feudal aristocracy found itself in conflict with a bourgeoisie, which was not privileged since it belonged to the Third Estate. The aristocracy was becoming more of a caste, and more exclusive in its privileges, whilst at the same time it was ruining itself by extravagance, by shutting itself off from the main process of money-making and, most serious of all, it was a class which was not renewing itself demographically. The bourgeoisie, on the other hand, was shown to be a class which was becoming more important within the State, which was continually growing in wealth as demand and production grew, which was naturally becoming more self-confident, and therefore more consciously resentful of its unprivileged status. Thus there was a clear and simple framework of generalization within which the Revolution was to be understood. But the work of modern scholars has made it increasingly difficult to accept this way of looking at things. It is impossible now to speak of either the aristocracy or the bourgeoisie in any meaningful way as a social class. The varieties of income and the diversities of ways of life both within the general category of aristocracy and within the general designation of bourgeoisie make it impossible to generalize about either. The nobility was sometimes becoming richer rather than poorer. The bourgeois, far from showing resentment against the noble, was sometimes able to emulate him, often by purchasing land and feudal rights, occasionally by purchasing a title. In these and other ways the suggestion that there was a fundamental struggle going on, between two social entities, becomes difficult to sustain. Historians are rather obliged to recognize a number of areas of social conflict and rivalry, a considerable complex of hostile and disparate interests, about which it is not easy to write in broad categories.

There is a tendency, therefore, to eschew generalizations, or to seek even wider ones, such as suggesting that the fundamental distinction in French society was that between rich and poor. But fortunately there do remain important elements of the crisis about which there is little or no disagreement among historians. It is clear that there were serious financial embarrassments. The general rise of prices which had taken place throughout the eighteenth century, the increase of Government expenditure (particularly on road works and on poor relief) and above all the cost of the four wars which France had waged between

1733 and 1783 had created a situation in 1788 whereby three-quarters of the State expenditure was being spent on servicing a huge national debt and on defence. A growing annual deficit threatened national bankruptcy. Yet what could be done? Expenditure could not be drastically reduced without touching the debt and thereby undermining public credit. The possibility of increasing indirect taxation was limited by the fact that indirect taxes were leased out to powerful financial agents, the farmers-general, in return for a fixed money payment which could only be increased once every six years. The possibility of increasing direct taxation implied the abolition of the fiscal exemptions enjoyed by the clergy, the nobility and middle-class office-holders and a radical reform of the machinery of tax collection. The whole financial question stressed the need to endow the Government with a proper budgetary system, that is to establish and define its powers. Thus any action which the Government might consider on a way of moving out of its financial difficulties would have meant administrative, social and political changes which were tantamount to revolution, and this was the experience of the reformers during the reign of Louis XVI.

In the light of this crisis and all that it involved, it is evident that there was a struggle for power. A set of choices was placed before all those who were politically conscious. For the first time it became necessary to define where power lay and to discuss who should rule. When the extent of the crisis was realized by 1787, then there was general talk of the need for reform, and there were hopes for national regeneration. It seemed that there had been both corruption and negligence at the centre of affairs. The rejection of the Government's plans for reform by the *parlements* and by the provincial Estates raised the question of privilege. It also underlined the confusions inherent in the organization of the *ancien régime*, which obstructed the tasks of administrators. It threw light on the belief, shared by all the *philosophes*, that the laws should rule, that they should be precisely formulated and that they should be interpreted by specialized judges.

The resistance of the *parlements* and the revolts of the nobility obliged the Government to announce that it was going to summon the Estates-General. And this news created a new aspect of the political struggle. The *parlements* and the provincial nobility had already amplified their protestations by deliberately stirring up popular riots and revolts. When the Parlement of Paris reassembled in September 1788 it did so amongst the cheering of the crowd and the ringing of church bells. But almost immediately it declared that when the Estates-General met, then it should be constituted and should meet as on the occasion of its last meeting in 1614. This meant that the First Estate (the clergy) and the Second Estate (the nobility) could always outvote the Third Estate, by two to one. Immediately there was an intensification of the political debate. Week after week pamphlets were published, attacking the privileged orders and demanding that the numbers of the Third Estate should be doubled and that voting should be by head. But the political debate was also widened. It was asked at whose expense the financial problem was to be solved. It was asked whether or not commoners were to be excluded from the most important positions in the army, the judiciary, the clergy. It was claimed that the Third Estate formed the most important part of the realm. Thus apprehension went with ambition; the political education of the Third Estate made great progress; and something equivalent to a revolutionary mentality was created.

This was not all. This agitation took place within a particular economic situation about which historians are in general agreement. The great mass of the population was, of course, the peasantry. Most of the peasantry were personally free and were not serfs; many peasants were the owner-occupiers of the soil. But within the great diversity of their conditions their situation was often precarious. The great majority of peasant landowners, and the majority of tenant-farmers and share-croppers, possessed only small holdings. They had sometimes to work as agricultural labourers or they had to engage in some form of rural industry. In addition there were large numbers, in some areas they could even be the majority, who owned no land at all and who were dependent upon earning wages. The rise of the population during the eighteenth century meant that there was increasing pressure on land and a growing demand for food; the general rise of prices adversely affected those who had little to sell and who often had to buy; the introduction of agricultural reforms which attacked common rights, the tightening-up of leases and the revival of many feudal claims were all further characteristics of the second half of the eighteenth century which made life more precarious for the rural populations. The whole situation worsened with an economic depression which coincided with the reign of Louis XVI. But the real disaster was the catastrophic harvest of 1788. From August of that year until July 1789, prices did not cease to rise. The importance of grain was such that these high prices absorbed the purchasing power of the urban communities, and helped to create industrial crisis, since production closely followed consumption. Thus, in 1788 and in 1789, when the political debate was reaching its climax, economic difficulties were at a maximum. There were grain and bread riots, in the countryside and in the towns; there was unemployment in the towns; it was impossible to collect taxes. And just as the political controversy generated its own myths and slogans, so starvation and acute distress produced their legends and rumours. Invariably it was the aristocratic class which bore the brunt of all obloquy.

The election to the Estates-General took place from the end of January 1789. France was divided into electoral districts formed out of bailli-wicks, the territorial divisions within which justice was traditionally administered. The deputies were elected in their separate orders. All bishops and parish priests could attend the electoral assembly of their order in the bailliwick and monks could send representatives. Lay nobles, aged twenty-five and over, could similarly attend their electoral assembly, either in person or by proxy. In both cases election was direct. Deputies of the Third Estate were chosen by a complicated system of indirect election. Except in Paris, where the vote was re-stricted to those who paid six *livres* in poll-tax, the franchise was almost universal, and those males aged twenty-five and over whose names were inscribed on the taxation lists were able to vote in their local assemblies. The election of their representatives then took place in two, three or four stages, according to the classification of the bailliwick. In December 1788 it had been finally decided that the Third Estate should have the same number of representatives as the clergy and nobility put together (but it was not settled how the orders should vote, whether by order or by head). Thus of the 1,165 deputies who were elected to the Estates-General nearly 600 composed the Third Estate.

The clergy had generally elected ordinary parish priests, only forty-six being bishops (and these including Talleyrand, who had recently been appointed Bishop of Autun, and Champion de Cicé, from Bordeaux, both reputed liberal). The majority of the nobility was made up of provincial aristocrats, but a group of about ninety (including Lafayette and Adrien Duport) were also liberal. In the Third Estate, lawyers and royal officials predominated, but their two most famous members were both men who had been elected out of their order, the Abbé Sieyes (who had published a highly successful pamphlet *Qu'est ce que le Tiers État?*) and the Comte de Mirabeau (also a pamphleteer, elected by Aix-en-Provence).

Louis XVI ceremonially received the three orders separately, at

Versailles on 2 May. He gave no indication of what decision he would take concerning the manner in which they would vote. But since he had been on the throne he had most distinguished himself by his uncertainty and his weakness. He had invariably given way to pressure and he had usually shown just sufficient obstinacy to offend all parties. On 4 May the Estates-General went in procession to the church of Saint-Louis. The deputies of the Third Estate were obliged to dress in plain black coats, whilst the clergy were in ceremonial robes and the nobles wore silk coats and plumed hats, and carried their swords. In the church the Bishop of Nancy presented the king with the homage of the clergy, the respects of the nobility and the most humble supplications of the Third Estate.

At last, the next day, the Estates-General began its work. After a vague and inconclusive address by the king, and an exhortatory (and largely inaudible) intervention by Barentin, the Garde des Sceaux, the longest and most important speech was made by Necker. This Swiss banker, who had been the Controller of Finance from 1777 to 1783 and who had presented a deliberately inaccurate account of the financial situation in 1781, had been recalled to power in August 1788. His reputation was considerable and Necker himself had always been at pains to encourage confidence in himself. But apart from announcing a reform of taxation, with the establishment of fiscal equality, and a few references to other areas in which there would be change, his speech was inconclusive. It made no mention of whether voting was to be by order or by head. Consequently, the next day, deputies from Brittany and from Dauphiné, areas where there had already been particularly lively refusals of royal authority and where political education must have been proceeding rapidly, took the lead in persuading the Third Estate that they should insist upon the Estates meeting in common. This attitude received the support of many of the clergy, but for about a month all the discussions had little effect other than maintaining excitement. It was not until 13 June that some members of the clergy joined the Third Estate, and not until 17 June that the Third Estate proclaimed itself the National Assembly. Then, the king having been greatly upset by the death of the Dauphin on 14 June and by the dynastic uncertainties which this had caused, it was decided to prevent the Assembly from meeting. The result was the Tennis Court oath, and some members of the nobility started to attend the Assembly. On 24 June the king gave way and invited the clergy and nobility to unite with the Third Estate. It seemed as if the Third Estate had gained a great victory.

All these events took place within the logic of their own development. Individuals were surprised by what was happening; no one had a clear-cut plan of reform any more than they had plans for revolution. But amongst the pressures which facilitated the victory of the Third Estate there was that of popular agitation. During April there had been an important riot in Paris when the house of a paper manufacturer called Réveillon had been sacked because he had been understood to suggest that wages should be reduced. Throughout May and June there had been widespread disturbances throughout the country and on 19 June the commander of the troops in the Paris region had stated that these incidents were unprecedented. Invariably, such manifestations encouraged the belief that there were many plots and conspiracies afoot. In the towns and in the countryside it was rumoured that the nobility was calling upon armies of brigands, foreigners and clerics, in order to maintain a shortage of grain and to crush the people. It was suggested that individuals such as the Duc d'Orléans, the king's rich cousin, were preparing to seize power. And it was inevitable that all these fantasies were linked to the inability of the Estates-General to start upon its reforming work. It was feared that the king and the nobility would seek to crush the Third Estate. A number of municipalities began to arm themselves; regular troops began to fraternize with the people.

It was therefore in the worst possible circumstances, after the National Assembly had turned itself into a Constituent Assembly, seeking to endow France with a constitution, that the king decided to restore his authority by force. He had been offended that Necker had not assisted him in his humiliating dispute with the Third Estate, but his dismissal of Necker on 11 July took place in an atmosphere of military indiscipline and bread queues in Paris. It seemed clear to the Paris population, when they learned of Necker's removal on Sunday, 12 July, that this would be followed by the dissolution of the Assembly. It was believed too that a further increase in the price of bread and national bankruptcy would necessarily accompany this event. There followed speech-making, demonstrations and insurrections. On 13 July customs barriers were burned, prisoners were set free, supposed stores of foodstuffs attacked, armourers' shops ransacked for arms and gunpowder. Drums were beaten, cannon were fired and the tocsin sounded as certain of those who had elected the members of the Third Estate sought to establish an organization which would control events. On Tuesday, 14 July, it was the prison of the Bastille which was attacked and captured, partly because it was hoped that arms would be found there, partly because this building seemed a sombre symbol of the authority which was now being contested. Several important officials were killed by the exultant crowd. As the news of the dismissal of Necker reached the provincial cities, such as Dijon, Rennes, Lyon, Nantes and Le Havre, there were similarly violent reactions.

Louis XVI then rejected the advice of those who told him to go to some garrison town. On 16 July he recalled Necker. The next day he went to Paris where the National Guard had been formed under the leadership of Lafayette and the astronomer Bailly (leader of the National Assembly). The king put the red and blue colours of the municipality of Paris next to the white cockade of the Bourbons. This *tricouleur*, and the fall of the Bastille, were to be the symbols of the Revolution. But a real revolution was taking place outside Paris. In the towns the municipal authorities either came to agreement with new revolutionary committees and their citizen guards, or were overthrown by them. In the countryside there were important risings which seemed to take on a certain unity in what has become known as 'The Great Fear'. The rumour of an aristocratic army or of brigands about to descend upon them and destroy the corn which was ripening in the fields and the constant realization of their own insecurity led to attacks on the châteaux, the burning of manorial rolls, the abolition of enclosures. If the professional men and the prosperous classes had seized power in the towns, there seemed to be a danger that rural France was falling into the anarchy of an enormous *jacquerie* which was a threat to all property. It was in order to meet the awkwardness of this situation that the deputies from Brittany, who used to concert policy together in the Breton Club (later to be called the Jacobin Club), decided that it would be politic to propose a voluntary renunciation of certain feudal privileges. On the night of 4-5 August, in an extraordinary session which got out of control, the privileges of nobles, tithe-holders and various institutions were abolished. It is true that subsequent sessions modified the decisions of this great occasion, and that, with the exception of personal services, the *status quo* remained in force until it could be decided which privileges had to be bought out and which were simply abolished. But no one can question the fact that 4 August represents a turning-point, since the social structure of the country was now being affected by a movement which had hitherto been political.

Thus it could be said that there were three revolutions in the course of 1789. That of the Third Estate which obliged the king to give way and which began the process of giving France a constitution; that of Paris and other French towns; and that of the countryside. The question has to be asked whether it is possible to see in any of these revolutions any sign of an organized conspiracy or plot, which would give some sort of overall explanation to events. Thus it was suggested by contemporaries, and the legend has not died, that the Duc d'Orléans was prominent in creating riots in the capital and tensions in Versailles. It has been claimed that the rising of 14 July was organized and paid for by bankers who feared a declaration of national bankruptcy on Necker's dismissal. Part of the *Grande Peur* is the repeated stories of horsemen riding into some village with stories of brigands and marauders being on their way and then riding off, presumably to spread the same panic elsewhere. But it is impossible to lend any credence to the idea of a vast conspiracy. It is true that the deputies of the Third Estate maintained political excitement high in Paris and other towns by their reports of the struggle of the Third Estate against the king and the privileged orders and that this was a new element in political life. It is true too that the Duc d'Orléans tried to profit from the situation and that the closing of banks and counting-houses made a number of individuals available for the happenings of 13 and 14 July. Within the Third Estate certain deputies, especially those from Brittany, guided their colleagues at certain crucial moments. But no one was in charge of events. Often, as in the case of Mirabeau, deputies appeared more daring in terms of language and tactics than they were in terms of ideas or intentions. The outstanding fact was that an original form of political crisis was working itself out against the background of a traditional form of agricultural crisis. It was easy to believe that there were aristocratic plots to get rid of the Third Estate and to starve the people into submission. Thus the isolated and sporadic urban and rural violence that had occurred throughout the spring took on a new dimension and was fanned into a movement of major revolt by the political crisis.

The revolutions of the Third Estate and of Paris and the major towns were extremely self-conscious. Perhaps it was the extraordinary procedure of summoning the Estates-General which caused those who were taking part in these dramas to feel that they were engaged in events of great historical significance. And a sign of this self-consciousness was the number of times that observers believed that the Revolution was over. When the king gave way and allowed the three orders to sit together on 27 June, Arthur Young wrote that the whole business was over and the Revolution was complete. After 14 July another English observer in Paris, Dr Rigby, spoke of the importance of what had happened 'with but a few days' interruption to the common business of the place', and at the end of the month Gouverneur Morris was also writing that the Revolution was complete. Such an impression was in no way surprising. For all the differences that separated the men of the Estates-General from one another it did seem that the victorious Third Estate was agreed upon its ultimate objectives. They wanted a government which would be rationally organized and which would not be arbitrary; they believed that those who were important in the community should have access to political power; they believed that what was good for one part of France should be good for another and they wanted government to be national rather than particular. In their attack upon ancient privileges they were self-interested and they were in no way democratic. But they were also moved by considerations of humanity and by their belief that they were accelerating the progress of mankind. The fact that the country was in the hands of these moderate, property-loving believers in a balanced constitution, like the fact that the harvest of 1789 was fair, seemed to suggest that the dangers were past. 1790 was to be called 'l'année heureuse'.

But, in fact, political stability was to prove elusive. Fundamental to any new system was the king. Distrust of him, of his queen Marie-Antoinette and of various other influences at Versailles was all the greater because his brother, the Comte d'Artois, and other nobles had emigrated from July onwards and were contributing to the suggestion that the French throne was only suffering a temporary embarrassment. In October certain military manifestations at Versailles created rumours of a royal coup. In reply, insurgents in Paris stormed the town hall (Hôtel de Ville) and then set out for Versailles. This uprising was mainly composed of women and it seems to have been organized. At all events it seems possible that neither Lafayette nor Bailly disapproved of the fact that both the royal family and the Assembly left Versailles for Paris. But from this time onwards the court was completely hostile to the Revolution, and its chief activity was to find some way of escaping from a situation which appeared to be intolerable. From this time onwards, too, the Revolution was to be dominated by Paris. Already political life in Paris had qualities of its own. The presence of a lively press and of influential orators, conflicts between Parisian workmen and their employers, the inexperience of the municipal authorities and the vital tradition of the Paris mob's power meant not only that both the enthusiasms and the suspicions that had been essential to the Revolution so far were sustained, but that there was a turning to new and more humble sections of the population.

Disturbances did not cease. There were continued movements in some towns against the high price of bread, some *parlements* challenged the power of the Assembly, there were parts of France where the peasantry continued to attack châteaux and to reclaim common land, there were serious conflicts between soldiers and their officers. To some extent the new system of local government increased the tension, since power was in the hands of an electorate based upon property qualifications. It elected officers (who were also eligible through their ownership of property), but they were without experience, there was no adequate machinery for linking their activities with the work of the central government, they had no financial resources, and they seemed to come into conflict with the poorer sections of the population.

However, the greatest cause of concern remained financial. The financial crisis which had been the basic reason for the summoning of the Estates-General in the first place still awaited solution, and had only been exacerbated by the breakdown in the collection of all taxes during the spring and the summer of 1789. The Assembly tried orthodox means, such as long-term and short-term loans, patriotic taxes and even the organization of gifts to the State. But when they had all failed they were forced to resort to a more dramatic act. It was claimed that the land and property of the Church belonged to the general community of believers, that is to the nation as a whole. If the State were to take over financial responsibility for the Church, then it could sell Church property, and this would not only solve its financial problems, it would also administer a great incentive to the economy since land would come on to the market and be available for new developments. The nationalization of Church lands was voted in December 1789, with little opposition, although there were those who declared that it was an attack on private property. The Civil Constitution of the Church whereby the State assumed responsibility for the clergy became law in July 1790, and in November the clergy were asked, as public servants, to take an oath of allegiance. These measures aroused violent resistance and more than half of the clergy refused to take the oath. Whilst awaiting the actual sale of the Church lands, negotiable bonds called *assignats* were issued, based upon these lands. For the time being these *assignats*, which were soon to be used as a form of paper money, maintained their value, but by the summer of 1791 the process of devaluation had begun.

Thus the measures concerning the Church were amongst the most important of the Revolution. Men went further than they had realized towards taking decisions in the name of the nation. A centre of opposition which included both the nobility and humble people was formed. A source of economic instability had been created. These factors have tended to outweigh the Declaration of the Rights of Man, voted in August 1791 (which guaranteed equal treatment before the law), the Constitution of 1791 (which gave greatest weight to an Assembly elected by the wealthiest citizens, probably well over four millions) and the thoroughgoing reform of the legal system which the Constituent Assembly began. Other reforms have also been overlooked such as the abolition of the venality of offices and a mild democratization of both the army and the navy.

The next phase of the Revolution was to bring France into closer contact with the rest of Europe and to destroy any belief that it was complete, or that the country could settle down. Whilst the Comte d'Artois and other émigrés openly urged a foreign invasion of France and worked for a civil war which would restore the old order (and maintained unrest in certain parts of France, especially in the south), the king decided to leave Paris and seek the protection of loyal troops in eastern regions. In June 1791 the king (and the royal family) were arrested at Varennes and brought back to Paris. It was impossible to go on as before. Whilst the moderates spread the fiction that the king had been 'kidnapped', a great impetus was given to the formation of popular societies and to more extremist clubs by their desire to dethrone and to try the king. It was at this time that those who were to be called sans-culottes first appeared. When the Constituent Assembly gave way, in October 1791, to the new Legislative Assembly, the problem that was most to the fore was still that of the dangers to France which resulted from émigrés and foreign courts. Although at the Jacobin Club Robespierre opposed the idea of solving this problem by starting a war, yet there were others led by Brissot who began to think that this was desirable. Other politicians believed that the political deadlock in which France had found herself would be resolved by a short and successful war, and that the crown would be able to resume its rightful place in the constitution. There were still others who looked forward to a French defeat and to the king being rescued. The result was the French declaration of war against Austria on 20 April 1792.

Almost immediately it was clear that the French army was not in a position to fight. An offensive misfired and Paris lay apparently open to the enemy (Austria and Prussia). The enemy was not only on the French frontiers; the enemy was also to be found in the counter-revolutionary forces which had come alive once war had been declared, particularly in the south. The decline in the value of the *assignat* led to the interruption of the normal processes of exchange, and many parts of France began to grow short of food. Once again there was suspicion that there had been a great betrayal of the Revolution and of the country. The forty-eight local constituency divisions of Paris, the sections, set up a revolutionary Government of Paris, the Commune. On 10 August 1792 they invaded the royal palace and imprisoned the king. The moderate Government found that it was obliged to summon a new Assembly, the National Convention, this time to be elected by universal suffrage. A Jacobin, Danton, who was working with the Commune, became Minister of Justice, the journalist Marat proclaimed that only through violence would the poor gain any benefits. But a few days later the Prussian army crossed the French frontier.

10 August 1792 was in many ways like 14 July 1789. But the French Revolution had changed in character. Up to 10 August the Revolution had been moderate and it had been legal. The people, whether in Paris and the towns or in the countryside, had played a vital part. But the representatives of the Third Estate had always been in charge. There had been little which was democratic or socialist; much of the work of the Third Estate had been to make a society where the economy would be free, where producers would be unhampered by tradition, privilege or arbitrary government. A law passed in 1791 protected these producers by forbidding all forms of association by capital or labour, thus attacking the guilds and preventing working-people from assembling together. But this liberal spirit could not survive the sort of crisis which the war was creating. French resources were scattered, so that an invading enemy did not have any easy target, but it was necessary for a French Government, organizing its defence, to mobilize the whole nation, its army, its supplies, its morale. It became necessary to control the movement of goods and to limit the rise of prices. Since the enemy was inside the frontiers of France as well as outside it was necessary to root out the enemy within, to find the traitors, to identify those whose opinions and interests seemed to clash with those of the nation as a whole. Because the Revolution had become popular it was

to take the form of endless meetings, demonstrations, debates, resolutions. In September 1792 there was the first manifestation of the Terror, when those suspected of having sympathy with the enemy received summary justice. From this time onwards the emphasis was on patriotism and the need to defend the Revolution by all means. Since the ordinary man was playing his part in all this, the ordinary things of life were changed too. People no longer addressed each other as 'Monsieur', they called themselves 'Citoyen', they addressed each other familiarly (*tutoiement*), they affected the careless dress of the *sans-culotte*, the names of the streets were changed into names showing the sovereignty of the people.

Thus the Revolution was no longer moderate, liberal and legal. The Revolution could be dictatorial, extreme, social and unpredictable. The change could be symbolized by the change in the role of Robespierre, the lawyer from Arras. As a deputy in the Third Estate he was distinguished by his humanity and his zeal for freedom. He wanted the under-privileged and the persecuted (such as actors and the Jews) to be protected; he wanted the death penalty to be abolished; he urged that justice should be reformed because it was better that a hundred guilty men should escape than that one innocent man should be condemned. But in this period of history Robespierre appears in a different light, as the most typical representative of a Government which was more powerful, more able to interfere in the private affairs of citizens, more organized in a great witch hunt so as to smell out the enemies of the Revolution, than any other Government in French history. This was not because Robespierre had changed in character. It was because the situation had changed.

And the crisis was prolonged. In September 1792 the French beat the Prussians at Valmy, in November they defeat the Austrians at Jemappes and their armies occupy Belgium, the left bank of the Rhine, Nice and Savoy. Danton proclaims a war of the peoples against the kings, and after the Republic has been proclaimed in France, Louis XVI is sentenced to death. 'You have not a sentence to give for or against a man', claims Robespierre, 'but a measure of public safety to take.' The king is executed in January 1793. But by February France is at war with a coalition that includes England, Prussia, Austria, Spain and Piedmont. The French armies are defeated in Holland and the French general goes over to the enemy. In the west of France there is an anti-Revolutionary rising in Anjou, which spreads to Brittany, Maine and Normandy. The rise in prices leads to insurrection in the towns. The Government attempts to maintain its hold on affairs; it establishes a revolutionary tribunal to try suspects ('soyons terribles, pour dispenser le peuple de l'être' is Danton's advice); it sends its representatives into the departments to organize the mobilization of an enormous army; it passes laws confiscating the property of aristocrats, fixing the value of the *assignat*, putting a ceiling on the price of corn and flour; it establishes a Committee of Public Safety. But it remains suspect, and after some initial failures on Sunday, 2 June 1793, yet another Parisian rising expels the Government from the Tuileries, and France finds itself in the grip of civil war.

The moderates who were evicted in this rising have commonly been called the Girondins, because Brissot and some of his followers came from the department of the Gironde, and it was they who largely dominated the Government since the meeting of the Legislative Assembly. However, it would be wrong to suppose that the Girondins formed a coherent or organized political party. They represented rather a group of individuals, romantic in their oratory, idealistic in their adherence to the principles of 1789, conceited in their conviction that they were destined to lead the country, who were fearful of carrying the Revolution forward. They suspected every increase in governmental power, they were reluctant to introduce further measures of reform, they feared as they deplored movements of the crowd. Behind the principle of this refusal to accept the creation of a Government which could be tyrannical, and sometimes more important than it, were questions of personality. The rivalry between Girondins and Jacobins was that of rival factions, but since the Jacobins were not in power they naturally became associated with the need for more effective action and therefore with the need for a strong Government which would save the Revolution. The Jacobins were prepared to work with the masses and with the *sans-culottes* of the Paris sections, and this was what was finally achieved on 2 June. But elsewhere in France, the moderates found support. There were movements in towns such as Lyon and Marseille which overthrew the Jacobin municipalities. After 2 June this movement was encouraged by Girondin fugitives and by a general refusal of provincial France to accept what had happened in Paris. Moderates who believed that the sovereignty of the nation had been violated joined with the royalists, the non-juring Catholics, the constitutional monarchists, in their opposition to Paris. Those who were wealthy and who had property to protect looked with apprehension at what was happening in Paris and with sympathy at the armies which were being raised, particularly in the south and in Normandy, to fight for this cause. The insurrectionaries in the west were being successful, they had captured Saumur on 9 June and they were reported ready to march on Paris. A French army was besieged in the Rhineland, and an allied army was advancing from the north of France.

Nor was the Government secure in Paris. The sections were disappointed that their demands for more direct control of government and for the creation of a more revolutionary army were not met. There was the danger of further insurrection. During this period the Committee of Public Safety was dominated by Danton, who in spite of his fiery oratory and massive appearance sought to meet all the dangers by a policy of compromise. He and his colleagues went particularly out of their way to reassure the peasantry, and abolished all remaining feudal dues without any compensation; the middle-class officials were placated by increases of salary; special representatives were sent to placate the provinces and to discredit the Girondins; a new democratic constitution was proclaimed. All these measures had some success. But they did not solve the problems created by high prices, shortage of food and a devalued money. Jacques Roux, a former constitutional cleric, denounced the laws which had been made by the rich and for the rich. It was pointed out that the constitution did not provide bread for those who had none and it was claimed that the Government had done nothing for the people. Bad news still came from the war and on 10 July Danton and his associates were not re-elected to the Committee of Public Safety. Three days later the dangers to the Revolution were emphasized by the murder of Marat, the journalist and orator and reputedly the friend of the people. Lyon was declared to be in a state of rebellion, certain Girondin and army leaders were accused of treason, measures against hoarders were announced, and it was thus in a tense and dangerous situation that Robespierre was called to become a member of the Committee of Public Safety.

It should not be thought that Robespierre was to dominate the Committee, any more than it should be thought that this Committee was the sole institution which governed France. There were other patriots and there were other revolutionary committees. But Robespierre had an influence which was particular. In so far as there were wide differences in ideas between the Jacobins and the *sans-culottes* it was necessary to find someone who would command respect amongst both. Robespierre seemed able to win the confidence of those who were attached to the Revolution as it had been conceived in 1789, and because of his undoubted patriotism, honesty and determination to save the Republic, he appealed to the *sans-culottes*. Since it was necessary to analyse and explain policy in the light of principles and ideas, then it was necessary to have someone in power who could express and define the philosophy of the Revolution. Robespierre was also by now experienced, and he had always been able.

In some ways the presence of Robespierre did not make any practical difference. Many of the important decisions had been taken before he became a member of the Committee (the decision to try Marie-Antoinette, for example). As before, some decisions were taken only reluctantly and as a result of *sans-culotte* pressure, such as that to enforce a *levée-en-masse* of all unmarried men between eighteen and twenty-five. But a new determination was apparent. The Terror became more effective in dealing with the supposed enemies of the State (both Marie-Antoinette and the Duc d'Orléans were executed). Churches were closed and a deliberate policy of dechristianization was launched. Prices were given a maximum, goods were requisitioned, wages were controlled. Festivities were organized to give the people confidence, and a Revolutionary calendar was adopted with the year One dating from 22 September 1792 so as to emphasize that a new era had dawned. What was perhaps more significant of Robespierre's power was that social reformers such as Roux (and the *enragés*) were imprisoned, and even the *sans-culotte* influence was reduced.

In practice the Committee of Public Safety had great success. By October Lyon was captured by the republican army and the important port of Toulon surrendered in December. The Vendéens suffered many reverses, and the Revolutionary generals won successes on all fronts. By 1794 there were nearly a million men under arms, and it was a member of the Committee of Public Safety, Lazare Carnot, who was known as the organizer of victory. In March and April 1794 Robespierre was able to send both Hébert and his left-wing followers and Danton and some of his friends who were financial speculators to the guillotine. In June the great battle of Fleurus opened Flanders to the French army and it was clear that the Republic was no longer fighting a defensive battle but had taken the offensive. The climax of the Revolution was over, yet Robespierre did not seem able to let up. In June and July there were 1,285 people condemned to death. He was associated with the Cult of the Supreme Being, a naturalistic, 'rational' religion which offended many of his followers. He had alienated many of his supporters among the people of Paris; there was jealousy and fear of the

Committee of Public Safety, and in the Convention there were many who regarded Robespierre with apprehension. He did little to defend himself and showed no sign of wanting to change his policies. It was simple to organize a conspiracy against him and on 26 July 1794 he was arrested and, later, executed.

The French statesman and historian Guizot was often to recall that he could remember seeing his mother kneel down and give thanks when she learned of the death of Robespierre. It was perhaps inevitable that he should have become the symbol of this period in Revolutionary history when the most extreme measures had to be taken in order to save the Republic. But the ease with which he was overthrown is also significant. It demonstrates how the Revolution was invariably controlled by those who were moderate, and most of whom were probably satisfied with a constitutional monarchy or with a bourgeois Republic. The ideals of the *sans-culottes*, who wanted each man to have his small piece of property, who wanted to control the politicians, who wanted goods to be plentiful and at a reasonable price, were irrelevant to the Revolution except in moments of unusual crisis. The *sans-culottes* represented an institutionalized popular movement, and since it was always possible that their sectionary societies could be stifled by the Jacobins, then there is something inevitable about their decline. And whilst it is true that the revolutionary crowds contained important elements of workshop masters, craftsmen, shop-keepers and small-traders who were able to formulate their ideas on the way in which society should be organized, it is impossible not to consider that the 'masses indigentes', the beggars, the unemployed and the ordinary workers played a most important part in the great days of the Revolution. At all events they were usually activated either by immediate needs or by particular hatreds and suspicions, such as the hatred of the aristocracy or the suspicion of betrayal. At moments, perhaps the real characteristic of the revolutionary crowd was exaltation; but by its very nature this could only be a transitory affair. The decrees of March 1794 which distributed property amongst the poor were directed at the property of those whose loyalty was suspect. It was an example of the importance of patriotism, not an example of belief in socialism.

With the overthrow of Robespierre, the Revolution began to back-pedal. Those who had succeeded in getting rid of important national figures, and who were not themselves famous in any way, encouraged a general hostility, both in Paris and in the provinces, against those who had been governing France. There was perhaps a general feeling of exhaustion, so that the people of Paris or groups in the provinces were without their natural leaders. Those who had been imprisoned by Robespierre formed such a heterogeneous group that it was not possible for them, on their release, to take up any organized policy other than that of revenge against those who had hitherto been in charge. Throughout the country there were those who took the opportunity to settle old scores, and in Paris a form of opulent and extravagant youth made its appearance. There were areas where a Counter-Terror was organized, and in many parts of the south the Jacobins were massacred. Elsewhere there were hesitations and intrigues, just as there continued to be popular demonstrations. But in November 1794 the Jacobin Club was closed down and preparations were under way to get rid of the assemblies of the sections. Most typical was the abolition of all price control, the abandonment of the attempt to stabilize the value of the *assignat* and the issue of more paper money. In April and May 1795 the *sans-culottes* rose against these conditions. It was to be their last rising and it was unsuccessful. Several thousands were imprisoned in the repression which followed, and it was clear that Paris could easily come under military control. However the real enemy, in 1795 as it had been for the Girondins, was strong central government. So when the Convention legislated to end its own existence by a new constitution, it established as its executive a five-man Directory. The franchise was limited to those who were wealthy, and there was a complicated system whereby there were annual elections and a constant apprehension that every year would bring about some important change in the political complexion of the State. The point really was that with the death of Robespierre and with the move towards the moderates and the persecution of Jacobin revolutionaries it seemed that the political options of the country remained open. It appeared possible that royalists would recover their position, and there were those who believed that the cause of social revolution was not irretrievably lost either. The closing stages of the Convention were marked by a rising of Parisian royalists in October 1795 (the rising of Vendémiaire) which was crushed by General Bonaparte; royalists were prominent and successful in electoral matters and they had an important and fashionable centre in the Rue de Clichy, so much so that in September 1797 General Augereau intervened and deported a number of deputies and journalists, whilst measures were taken against royalists and priests; in May 1796 'the conspiracy of equals' led by Babeuf attempted to put in practice a more thoroughgoing social revolution, based upon a redistribution of wealth, but the leaders were arrested before they could accomplish anything. Thus there were political oscillations and an atmosphere of plot and counter-plot. But the Directory survived. Too much attention has probably been placed upon the relaxation of morals and the search for pleasure which is to be found in Parisian society at this time. Barras (famous because of his friendship with Bonaparte) was exceptional as a Director who was cynical and corrupt; the other Directors were sincerely republican and devoted to the Revolution as it had existed in its earlier stages. They were opposed to the monarchy, the aristocracy and the Church, and they sought, through education and through a systematic cult of patriotic republicanism, to create a stable and humane society. Once again, power lay with those who were wealthy and was not affected by the fact that in the last five years of the century there were many *nouveaux riches*. As a historian has put it, the Directory represented an attempt to govern normally in abnormal circumstances.

What particularly marked the Directory was its foreign policy. Although by 1795 the Revolutionary wars against Prussia, Holland and Spain had been concluded satisfactorily for France (which had annexed Belgium), war continued against Austria, particularly seeking the conquest of northern Italy. This war, in which Bonaparte became the commander, was to be explained in many ways. For example the economic situation remained poor and there was still no satisfactory means of exchange. There were those who hoped that the plunder of Lombardy and Tuscany would solve the financial problems of the Government. But there was probably a more general consideration. Patriotism remained a great unifying factor; few Governments felt strong enough to make peace and to dispense with military victories. The result was Arcola (1796) and Rivoli (1797) and a peace treaty which gave France the left bank of the Rhine and which created the Cisalpine Republic out of the conquered lands of northern Italy. The expedition to Egypt followed, seeking to make Egypt into a French colony and to destroy British commerce. The result was the coalition of 1799, which brought England, Russia, Turkey and Austria against France, and which threatened a new invasion and a new crisis.

It was natural enough that this provoked a new wave of Jacobinism. The Directors (and by this time Sieyès was one of them, so that the Revolution seemed to have come full circle) declared that they were willing to take measures of public safety yet they did not wish to see a revival of the Revolutionary committees and the spirit of 1793. But patriotic Jacobins retorted that the Directors were afraid of using 'that omnipotent force' which was the people and that they feared the mass of republicans more than they feared the invaders. All sorts of accusations of treason were present and the situation was made more complicated by royalist risings, notably a serious affair in the south-west which began in August 1799, and by a revival of activity in Brittany. It was in this situation that Bonaparte decided to abandon his army in Egypt and return to France. It is true that by the time he reached Fréjus (9 October 1799) Masséna had won military victories in Switzerland and the immediate threat of invasion had disappeared. But the war would begin in the spring; the political predicament would return in some form or another; the economic crisis remained strident. The idea of 'arranging' for Bonaparte to seize power appealed to many politicians. A terrorist plot was invented and the stage was prepared, not without difficulty. Bonaparte played the part that had been assigned him, and on 10 November 1799 (18 Brumaire) he expelled the Assembly and took power into his own hands.

In December 1799 Bonaparte announced his new constitution. His language was curt, as he told his fellow citizens that the Revolution was over. But it is difficult to believe that the action of a number of bold republicans in bringing this general to the forefront had ended anything. Only if the Revolution is to be equated with certain days of excitement and popular action (usually in Paris) or if it is to be identified with the unusual circumstances and the fragile construction of 1793 or 1794 can Bonapartist rule be seen as the definitive ending of the Revolution. Still less can Bonaparte rule be seen as the triumph of what has sometimes been called the Counter-Revolution. Much has been made recently of the forces within France which opposed the Revolution and which, at certain times, opposed the Revolution by force of arms (such as the four departments of Brittany, Lyon or the Vivarais). It has been suggested that whilst this Counter-Revolution appeared particularly dangerous because it was supported by foreign powers which were France's enemies, in reality the Counter-Revolution was largely a French phenomenon in which the main trends of the Revolution were opposed. It could take the form of a large peasant revolt or it could be urban, but it was invariably opposed to the centralization, rationalization and anti-clericalism which appeared to be the most important parts of the Revolution. There was bound to be an aggravation of all sorts of local issues when the Revolution introduced its governmental system; there were bound to be local resentments when the central government called for conscripts. It is difficult to make this into a movement having its own ideology and which saw with satisfaction the establishment of Bonaparte's anti-democratic regime. In terms of principles (though possibly not in terms of the individuals concerned), the Counter-Revolution saw that Bonapartism was a continuation of the Revolution and perhaps we would be well advised to see it in the same light.

The Empire

The Revolution had not produced men of outstanding quality. Mirabeau had not been trusted; Lafayette proved himself to be shallow; Danton's pre-eminence was probably more apparent than real; Robespierre had not been able to adapt himself to changing events. It is natural therefore that historians should see the arrival of Bonaparte on the scene as an event of particular significance. History is always more easily explained if it is seen in terms of an individual. And Bonaparte seemed to have considerable talent as well as considerable ambition. Not only did he seek to rule France himself but he seemed to have the ability to do so. He was energetic, he could work long hours without apparent signs of fatigue, he had a remarkable memory, he had a clear mind which could grasp what was essential in any discussion. Generally speaking too he was free from any ideology, and could approach affairs cynically and practically. It is not surprising that he can be quoted as saying many contradictory things at different times. But he had many limitations. He was over-loyal to his family (which was not always loyal to him) and the Bonapartist 'clan' was a source of weakness. He was too dominated by the Mediterranean and did not appreciate the importance of other seas, the Baltic and the Atlantic. He was too peremptory and did not always realize that his interventions in administrative matters often created confusion rather than efficiency. He was a gambler, invariably ready to risk everything on the outcome of a single battle. Above all, he was always in a hurry. He never had time to prepare a campaign, he seldom had the opportunity to reflect, he sometimes could do little more than initiate measures which he could not follow through, in spite of his passion for detail. In a sense the Empire was an improvisation and it is ironical that certain of its institutions proved to be particularly lasting. It hardly seems that Napoleon himself had much impression that his rule would be a long one. In his talkative self-centredness he often remarked that there were many generals who thought they had as good a claim to power as himself or that, unlike a king or an emperor, he had only to suffer a single defeat and all would be lost for him. Perhaps he was always essentially a soldier, and just as it was the speed of his troop movements which disconcerted his adversaries, so in politics it was his incessant and rapid activity which allowed him to keep the initiative.

At first it is the continuity with the preceding regime which is most obvious. Bonaparte was a republican and a patriot. Just as he had told the Austrians with whom he had negotiated in Italy that the French Republic existed like the sun in the heavens, so he extolled the principles of the Republic, and it was always recognized that his power had emerged out of the Revolution. The *coup d'état* with which he was associated, after all, had had its predecessors under the Directory. The constitutional arrangements (and Bonaparte maintained the Revolutionary calendar, speaking about the 'Constitution de l'An VIII') were as complicated as those of the Directory, with different assemblies and means of election. The desire for conciliation was even more marked than under the preceding regime, and Bonaparte took the initiative in granting individual pardons, revising the lists of those who had been exiled, encouraging both royalists and Jacobins to rally to him and to 'wear the uniform of Bonaparte', seeking a religious pacification. But there was also a new element: that of the State's authority as interpreted by Bonaparte. His most significant departure was from the role which some of those who had organized the *coup d'état* had thought of giving him, that of a presiding *roi fainéant*. Bonaparte became First Consul (with Cambacérès, a legal specialist, and Lebrun, a financial expert and formerly secretary to Chancellor Maupeou, as Second and Third Consuls) and alone had the power to appoint to the Council of State, nominate officials, propose and promulgate laws. Authority became concentrated in the one man, and as the constitution was frequently revised, so its revisions were always in the direction of reducing popular control over matters of State. His method of exercising this authority was also noticeable. He had always encouraged propaganda around his person and this was continued. In January 1800 the liberty of the press was abolished and all newspapers which could be classified as political were suppressed (so that whilst there had once been seventy-nine newspapers in Paris, eventually, as the Government became progressively more severe, there were only four). Censorship was extended to theatres. The administrative reform of 1800 established a rigid centralized system, with the departments presided over by the prefects, the *arrondissements* by the sub-prefects, the communes by the mayors. The judicial reforms of 1800 established a similar hierarchy for the administration of justice, presided over by the Minister of Justice, and the Code Civil (which was not completed until 1804) established authority as the legal principle of social life: the authority of the father over the children, of the husband over the wife, of the employer over the employees. And whilst Bonaparte showed his readiness to conciliate, he was prepared to oscillate between conciliation and repression, and in the west there were times when his forces showed a brutal determination in their suppression of dissident groups.

No one can believe that Bonaparte's success is to be explained only by his talents. It probably corresponded to a certain moment in the life of France when there was a need for the security of strong government and possibly even a turning against the parliamentary government of the Directory. Bonaparte guaranteed the conquests of the Revolution. Those who had bought the lands of the Church or who had acquired land taken from émigré noblemen were assured that they could keep this land. There was no possibility of restoring aristocratic rights or privileges, no question of reviving the ecclesiastical tithe. With the foundation of the Bank of France in 1800, Bonaparte conciliated a number of powerful private bankers and later endowed this institution with the right to issue paper money based upon gold deposits. Thus with an alliance between private capital and the Government and a reform of the tax-collecting system, the State's finances began to be healthy; with a reliable means of exchange economic life could become normal. When supplies of food ran short in 1800 Bonaparte organized the purchase of wheat abroad, whilst the Prefect of Police in Paris built up stocks, controlled prices, established a corporation of bakers; any rioters, whether in Paris or the provinces, were ruthlessly dealt with. Meanwhile abroad Bonaparte won the victory of Marengo in June 1800 and it seemed that there could be no foreign menace to France. It was therefore as if there was a wide vested interest in maintaining Bonaparte's rule. With customary shrewdness Bonaparte saw this and in September 1800 he at last replied to the exiled Louis XVIII (the brother of Louis XVI, Louis XVII the Dauphin having died in 1795) who had twice written in the hope of persuading him to become a royalist. A royalist restoration, he said, would mean 100,000 corpses. Louis XVIII, he suggested, could not hope to return to France in such conditions and he should sacrifice his interests to the repose and the welfare of France. Part of the essence

of Bonapartist rule was the suggestion that a page had definitively been
turned in the history of France.

With this there was propaganda. Bonaparte consolidated his position
with military communiqués which surrounded his person with an aura
of successful glory. And there was also patronage. Bonapartism meant
official posts. The Senate, the Legislative Corps, the Tribunate, the
Council of State, the Ministers, prefects, a growing administration –
all meant vacancies right at the beginning of the regime. Bonaparte was
able to conciliate a host of the most politically conscious classes, and
this was a task for which his excellent memory, his cynicism and his
desire both to be and to appear powerful constituted the perfect equipment. It should be noted that he did not favour those who were particularly humble. The best means of gaining employ from Bonaparte
was to be serving the State already, or to have a father who was serving
the State. In this way Bonaparte was able to make use of administrators
who were experienced; but he was also able to reinforce his own position amongst the political élite. In addition Bonaparte used the immense
resources of the State as a means of bribery. Diplomats, generals and
statesmen throughout the period of the Consulate and Empire received
huge gifts of money as well as honours. Thus the system whereby one
man established an authority which was based upon the administration,
the army, the notables and a vague general consent gradually established itself.

The Treaty of Lunéville in February 1801 brought peace between
France and Austria and confirmed French possession of Belgium and
the Rhine frontier, whilst Italy (except for Venetia) passed under
French influence (in 1802 Bonaparte became President of the Italian
Republic). In March 1802 the Peace of Amiens was signed with
England. The year 1802 also saw some significant developments at
home. An amnesty was accorded to the émigrés and such lands as had
not been confiscated were given back to them. A new form of school,
the lycée, was created; a new form of decoration, the Legion of
Honour, was instituted; slavery which had been abolished by the Revolution was reinstated in the French colonies; the Concordat which had
been signed with the Pope in 1801 (and in which the Pope had recognized the First Consul's right to appoint bishops and the First Consul
recognized the bishops' rights to appoint priests) was followed by the
Government's publication of the organic articles on the Catholic religion which controlled many of the external aspects of church life
(ecclesiastical dress, the ringing of church bells, etc.). Most telling of all,

Bonaparte suggested that the French people should be consulted on whether or not he should become Consul for life. With three and a half millions voting in favour of this, over a period of three months, and with only a few more than 8,000 voting against, Bonaparte was proclaimed Consul for life in August 1802 with the right to appoint his successor. 15 August 1802, Napoleon's thirty-third birthday, was celebrated as a national holiday, and in 1803 his effigy appeared on the coins. France had become a monarchy again.

In May 1802 Bonaparte put a crippling duty on all British colonial goods and believing that England was vulnerable to this sort of economic warfare began to encourage French production and trade. He maintained his troops in Holland in spite of the Treaty of Amiens. He intervened in Switzerland to weaken the federal government. He sent missions to Egypt, Syria, Turkey and India. In Italy he annexed Elba, Piedmont and Parma. Finally he insisted that England should evacuate Malta and that, on the English refusal, it was England which was responsible for the outbreak of war. But the outbreak of war seemed to point to a crisis in the State. There were generals who were jealous of Bonaparte's power, notably Moreau; there were royalists in the west and in Paris who were in league with the British. The presence of the Bourbon prince the Duc d'Enghien in the neutral state of Baden seemed to be linked to these conspiracies about which there were many rumours. Bonaparte had him seized and shot in March 1804. In May it was declared that the Government of France was entrusted to an emperor. A plebiscite gave overwhelming support to this decision and in December, in the presence of the Pope, Napoleon crowned himself and the empress, Joséphine. The execution of the Duc d'Enghien meant that there was a definitive break between Napoleon and the royalists. Cynical royalists commented that they had hoped to have a king, but they had created an emperor.

If the Empire coincided with a European crisis, this crisis was to be prolonged. A new coalition was formed against the emperor and soon war was continuous. In Bavaria Napoleon won the battle of Ulm, in Moravia that of Austerlitz, in Saxony Jena, in eastern Prussia Eylau, in West Prussia Friedland. By 1807 Napoleon had come to an agreement with the Tsar at Tilsit, he had reorganized Germany into a confederation of the Rhine, the Grand Duchy of Warsaw was virtually governed by a French general, Switzerland and Italy were distributed to Napoleon's family and associates, and an economic blockade against England from Brest to the Elbe was being organized. 15 August 1807 was a great fête of the Empire. Napoleon was at the apogee of his power. From this time onwards it is possible to see a decline: after Portugal had refused to join in the blockade of English goods, Napoleon intervened unsuccessfully in Spain and Portugal; at home both Talleyrand and the Minister of Police, Fouché, considered replacing him by Murat; in 1808 Napoleon ordered the occupation of Rome and subsequently had the Pope arrested, thereby destroying the good relations with the Catholics; a fifth coalition was formed against France and with the sending of a British force to the Low Countries and with the British fleet in liaison with the royalists in the south of France, it looked as if there was an intrigue to replace Napoleon by another general, Bernadotte, which was only broken by Napoleon's victory against the Austrians at Wagram (1809). Conscious of the fragility of his system and desirous of having an heir, he divorced Joséphine and married Marie-Louise, the daughter of the Austrian emperor, in 1810.

Napoleon's heir, called the king of Rome, was born on 20 March 1811. He was heir to an enormous empire, comprising nearly 43 million people, stretching from Rome to Lubeck, administered in 130 departments. Beyond them stretched the vassal states which through military and fiscal means were regarded as simple prolongations of France. But it was widely recognized that all this was a precarious inheritance. As the emperor grew more authoritarian, then the opposition to him, whether of individuals, of Catholics, of different sorts of royalists, of liberals, Jacobins or intellectuals, grew more intense amongst a popular hostility to continued taxation and conscription. When Napoleon left for the Russian campaign in 1812, an obscure and discredited general called Malet declared in Paris that Napoleon had been killed and announced the formation of a new Government. His attempt only lasted for a few hours, but it was enough to show that no one thought that Napoleon II could succeed. The disastrous Russian campaign was followed by further reverses in Germany (Leipzig, October 1813) and Italy, the loss of Spain and Holland and by the invasion of France at the beginning of 1814. Napoleon's victories against the allied armies (Brienne, Champaubert, Montmirail, Vauchamps, Montereau) were useless. The opposition of the liberals to him became vocal, the British occupied Bordeaux, the royal family returned to France. On 31 March 1814 the Tsar, the king of Prussia and their troops entered Paris, a provisional government was established under Talleyrand, and, deserted by his marshals, Napoleon abdicated on 5 April. A few days later he was given a pension for life and the tiny island kingdom of Elba, and after having met with further humiliations and some public hostility, he arrived in his exile at the beginning of May. It was an inglorious ending to the Empire.

The decision to recall the Bourbons to the throne of France was in no way a national decision. There was no movement of opinion in favour of the royal family, there was simply a number of intrigues in Paris. In these intrigues it was Talleyrand and the personnel of the imperial administration who were able to impose their views on the foreign sovereigns, especially the Tsar, who seemed to have the destiny of France under their control. The idea of Talleyrand and his associates was to safeguard their own positions and to impose upon the Bourbons the condition of a form of constitutional government. This manoeuvre was largely unsuccessful in the sense that once Louis XVIII had been proclaimed king (6 April), the fact that conditions were attached to the proclamation appeared insignificant. Louis XVIII left England two weeks after the proclamation and journeyed towards Paris with agonizing slowness; the temptation to go and pay homage to him was irresistible and many of those who had been most insistent upon imposing conditions openly accepted him as king. But Talleyrand's manœuvre was successful since on 2 May, just prior to entering Paris, Louis XVIII deemed it prudent to announce that he would be drawing up a form of constitutional government, whilst maintaining that such an act was voluntary on his part.

Thus began the Restoration. But whilst the greater part of the *notables*, the aristocracy, the Church, the political class, the officials, bankers, businessmen and intellectuals, accepted the return of the Bourbons with remarkable ease, there was little enthusiasm amongst the ordinary people. Soldiers disobeyed their officers and deserted in large numbers; unemployed workers demonstrated beneath the windows of the Tuileries palace; elsewhere a general indifference was reported. The outstanding feature of this Restoration was that within a short time the goodwill had been destroyed and the hostility had been intensified. This was partly the fault of the royal family and its advisers. They were often ignorant of the nature of the administration which they had inherited ('What is a department? What is a prefect?' wrote the king's brother, the Comte d'Artois, to the Minister of the Interior); they were divided, the moderate royalists finding themselves countered by more intransigent figures who wished to mark the ending of the Revolution by a more decided return to the *ancien régime*. The Government gave way on many matters. Sundays were to be observed as rest days. It became obligatory for houses to be decorated on certain saint-days, for officials to take part in certain religious processions. The anniversaries of the executions of Louis XVI and Marie-Antoinette were to be regarded as days of penitence and expiation, and this was even extended to include the Vendéen leader Cadoudal. Because the Restoration had inherited many debts, a high level of taxation had to be maintained (although the earlier royalist propaganda had promised a reduction of indirect taxes), many officials were sacked, officers put on half-pay, soldiers dismissed from the service. The magistrature was purged and a form of censorship was re-established. And the discontent caused by all this was heightened by the insistence with which returned émigrés demanded offices and positions. (It was said that one nobleman claimed to be made a Rear-Admiral since, having been a naval cadet in 1789, this would have been his rank had the Revolution not intervened. The justice of his claim was officially admitted but he was told that unfortunately he had lost his life at Trafalgar in 1804.) Most serious of all, in the countryside, the nobility in some cases claimed the return of their lands which had been bought (usually many years previously), and in many cases both they and the clergy demanded the revival of former privileges. Royalist newspapers and pamphleteers joined in this counter-revolutionary activity and although the Government protested, there were many rumours about the return of feudal obligations and the tithe.

It was in these circumstances that Napoleon, on Elba, received an emissary from France who assured him 'as a positive and undeniable fact' that the existing Government had lost the support of the people. There was no agreement amongst the critics of the Bourbons as to what should replace them, and those (such as Fouché) who were most anxious to have regular constitutional government would have preferred the proclamation of Napoleon II and a Regency. But characteristically Napoleon took a rapid decision and without any preparations he left Elba on 26 February, accompanied by a thousand soldiers. Having won over the first detachment of soldiers that he met, he encountered no opposition and travelling with remarkable speed he entered the Tuileries on 20 March, shortly after Louis XVIII had fled to Ghent.

If this resurrection of the Empire had been apparently simple, and explicable essentially in terms of Napoleon's boldness and swiftness, it is essential to see it also as a political move. Proclamations, which had been drawn up at Elba or during the journey at sea, were printed at

Digne and at Gap in the south-east, and distributed in considerable quantities. They were addressed essentially to the revolutionary and democratic sentiments of the people. They claimed that the Bourbons had attempted to make the army dependent upon the aristocracy and to restore feudalism to French society. At Grenoble he claimed that he had come to deliver France from 'the insolence of the nobility, the pretentions of the priests, and the yoke of the foreign powers'. Later he was to say that nothing had surprised him more on his return to France than the hatred of priests and nobles. He claimed that it was as widespread and as violent as at the beginning of the Revolution, and he clearly aimed to profit from it. In addition to restoring the *tricouleur* flag and reinstating many dismissed officials, his first decrees promised a constitution which would be in the interests and according to the will of the nation. In a message to the Conseil d'État he stated that sovereignty resided in the people and that this was the only legitimate source of power. Nevertheless he was anxious that the continuity of the Empire should persist, and when the new constitution was drawn up it was given the significant title of Acte Additionnel. It was also disappointing since it did not institute parliamentary government, as expected, but left the initiative of proposing laws to the emperor. When it was submitted to the approval of a national plebiscite there were literally millions of abstentions. When the first elections were held in May, it was liberals rather than Bonapartists who triumphed.

Thus Napoleon's return had created great excitement and he had appeared as the saviour of the Revolution. But within a short space of time support had waned. Rival political groups discussed the need for important changes in the future. There was a general feeling that Napoleon's return could only be temporary. Certain of his Ministers were in touch with royalists, whilst the Government appeared slow and strangely inefficient in many ways. An economic depression affected industry and trade. There was general apprehension concerning the length of the war, which the allied sovereigns had immediately declared. But the Belgian campaign only lasted four days. Napoleon was defeated at Waterloo on 18 June 1815, he abdicated on 22 June, and Louis XVIII returned to Paris on 8 July.

This Second Restoration was also the result of intrigues (this time Wellington joined Fouché and Talleyrand) and it was accompanied by considerable violence and by a large army of occupation. In the south, sometimes as soon as the news of Waterloo was learned, there were attacks against the Bonapartist personnel which frequently took the form of a spontaneous Terror, 'the White Terror' as it has been called. In some areas it spread beyond the royalist–Bonapartist struggle and became a Catholic–Protestant confrontation, and although order was restored by the arrival of Austrian troops, in November 1815 the reopening of the Protestant church at Nîmes gave rise to further violence. The presence of 150,000 foreign troops also gave rise to a sporadic agitation, and a whole number of incidents took place in which foreign troops were accused of destruction and pillaging, whilst French individuals were guilty of assassination and violence. In all these ways Napoleon's adventure of the Hundred Days (for when the king returned to Paris he was welcomed with the words, 'it is but a hundred days since your Majesty left us') was to leave an impressive mark on French history. The impression was given of a Bonapartism which was revolutionary, popular and liberal. The association between the Bourbons and the foreign powers was enforced, and the peace treaty not only reduced France to the limits of 1792, but removed Sarrelouis, Savoy, Philippeville and Marienburg and imposed a massive indemnity. Thus foreign policy was to become an important issue and it became normal to attack the treaty arrangements of 1815. Finally, although it seemed that there was a great consensus of opinion in France which was in favour of some liberal, bourgeois and moderate constitutional government, the Hundred Days indicated yet again that there was a fragility about power in the French State, that it was there for the taking, and that there was an underlying current of violence in French society which could cause savage conflict.

The Restoration and the July Monarchy 1815–1848

The population of France in 1815 was probably just short of thirty millions. To some extent the high birth-rate, which had been a characteristic of the *ancien régime* and which had given France a large and young population, had been maintained, and the persistence of military conscription for bachelors had encouraged early marriages (in 1813, for example, there had been an unusually large number of marriages in order to escape military service, and the birth-rate in 1814 had been high). But there are some signs that the increase had been checked. The numbers killed in the wars (perhaps 900,000), the growth of practices of birth-control, the fact that 1812 was a year when food was short and the typhus epidemic of 1813 were amongst the principal causes of this check. The 1820s, however, were to see a considerable increase, and by 1831 the population was over thirty-two and a half millions. It was probable that something like one-seventh of this population lived in towns with a population of 20,000 or over. There were only three towns that had a population of over 100,000: Paris, which by the beginning of the Restoration period had a population of just over 700,000, but where the rate of expansion seemed to slow down at the beginning of these years; Marseille and Lyon which had about 115,000 each. Towns such as Bordeaux and Rouen had populations in the neighbourhood of 90,000. It has been calculated that there were some twenty departments that possessed no town of more than 10,000 inhabitants, and that there were nearly 500 towns that had a population of between 2,000 and 3,000. Thus France was essentially a country dominated by agriculture and by a rural population.

For a long time it was assumed that this rural population had been responsible for a steady improvement in agricultural conditions and productivity. It was believed that only in this way was it possible for the countryside to support the continual growth of population, and that the legal changes of the Revolution, by freeing the peasant from many irksome obligations, had placed him in a situation where he could respond to the challenges and the opportunities of the market. It does not, in fact, seem that this was always the case. The class of enlightened peasants, with their small and medium-sized landholdings, who were able to transform certain regions, such as the Nivernais, does not seem to have been general. Because a great quantity of land was made available, the Revolution often encouraged the peasant to extend the amount of land he possessed, rather than to increase his productivity by improving his method of farming. There could be some reluctance amongst landowners to see tenants introduce new methods, and old feudal dues were sometimes incorporated in the new leases. Then, whilst some agricultural workers saw their wages rise during the Revolutionary and Napoleonic periods, it is true to say that many, whether peasant landowners, tenant-farmers or labourers, saw their economic situation become more precarious. Historians now prefer to put an emphasis on the diversity of agricultural conditions and to point out that just as the different geographical regions introduce a considerable variety into French agricultural life so the position of the rural population was bound to change from one part of France to another. There were some agricultural communities which were largely self-sufficient (except for supplies of salt and luxuries); there were others which were closely integrated with the economy of neighbouring towns; there were some areas which regularly sent labourers to work in the towns during the winter months; there were regions where it was customary to live on a wide variety of different foods, others which were dominated by a single (and often inferior) type of corn. Perhaps the only safe generalization that one can make about the rural population as a whole is its poverty. As Stendhal's hero Julien Sorel observed, most men could come home to their cottages on a winter's evening and find neither bread nor chestnuts nor potatoes there.

The most common way of supplementing income for the rural population was through industry. Rural industry had become widespread during the eighteenth century. It had been encouraged by the Government, entrepreneurs had been attracted by the cheaper wages they had been able to offer, and the manufacturers of new cloths had sometimes thought that they would be more successful with the newly found workers in the countryside. So important had the spread of rural industry become that there are examples of authorities forbidding industrial work during the harvest period. This had continued throughout the Revolutionary and Napoleonic years. But by 1815 industrial production had taken on different aspects. France had become more industrialized during the Empire. The drop in industrial production which had coincided with the Revolution had been stopped and until there was an industrial crisis in 1810-11, French industry was producing more than at the end of the *ancien régime*. This includes the building industry which had been stimulated by Napoleon's interest in public works, as well as textile, metallurgical and chemical industries. Factories equipped with modern machinery had been installed at great expense, and the use of steam-engines to drive the machinery meant that work was more regular and more intense. In towns such as Rouen, Lille or Mulhouse there was demand for women and children to work the machines and there was the need for specialist mechanics (who often came from England) to instal and service them. But the characteristic of French industry was the manner in which different forms of production existed side by side together, old and new. The cotton industry became largely mechanized by 1830, woollen much less so, linen and flax still less. The cost of products varied from one region to another, but they all feared English competition and demanded that there should be high protective tariffs.

French society of the Restoration was dominated by the political system. Louis XVIII had announced in 1814 that he would endow France with a constitution, and this royal concession, obviously granted by a monarch who was stressing his own benevolence and not admitting that his powers could be restricted or that sections of the population possessed rights, took on the medieval term of the Charter (*La Charte*). It created two houses of Parliament – the Peers who were created by the king and the lower house which was elected by a limited number of citizens. One's right to vote was judged by one's wealth, and in this calculation, by which less than 100,000 men were adjudged able to vote (and perhaps a tenth of these were eligible to be elected a deputy), the possession of land was more important than other forms of wealth. Thus the nobility tended to dominate the Chamber of Deputies and it was not uncommon for more than half of the deputies to be noble. The nobility had a dominant place in the administration and in the countryside, and the abolition of feudal rights and the confirmation of the sales of ecclesiastical and émigré lands during the Revolution did not remove their influence.

The political circumstances with which the Restoration began also emphasized the importance of the nobility. The first elections were held in the abnormal conditions of August 1815. About a third of those who had the right to vote abstained and there were considerable pressures on those who did vote. The result was the Chambre Introuvable, as it was called, in which an enormous majority of nobles and landowners expressed only one idea, their hatred of the Revolution and the Empire. They wished to punish those who had been prominent in support of the preceding regimes and they demanded indemnification for their property losses under the Revolution. It was as if they were returning to the aristocratic revolt of 1788 and seeking for a devolution of power towards the provinces in which they were the natural leaders. They found support for their ideas from the heir to the throne, the king's brother, the Comte d'Artois, who virtually set up an independent and parallel Government, and there were aristocratic and Catholic organizations throughout the country which sought to embody the ideals of this Counter-Revolution. Some 70,000 arrests were made, the administration was purged, more than 150 specially designated personalities were banished, and some generals who had gone over to Napoleon in 1815 were shot. Attempts were made to reconstitute the Church's wealth and it was suggested that the tithe should be reintroduced. Divorce was made illegal.

There was thus an atmosphere of conflict and repression which the king attempted to moderate. He dissolved the Chamber and a more moderate Parliament was re-elected in 1816. He matched plots with counter-plots, he chose as his Ministers those who were liberal and who were anxious to make the system work, he sought to place his government on a sound financial basis. Doubtless Louis had his reasons for this. He was shrewd; he did not want to be the prisoner of a rebellious aristocracy; he had a personal liking for the leading liberal of the time, Decazes; he was under pressure from foreign ambassadors. But in effect, he was appealing from the aristocracy to the section of the country which had profited from the Revolution, the bourgeoisie which was important in the central administration and the banking and financial groups which enabled the Government to pay off the indemnity and get rid of the occupying forces. These men had their connections with the *ancien régime*, and they had sometimes been important as moderate royalists under the Revolution or as officials under the Empire. They believed in national government, and they were opposed to the arbitrary, sectarian and violent measures which they saw advocated by the ultras. When the ultras, convinced that they represented popular opinion, became more democratic, then the moderates, who were far from believing in democracy, were all the more decided in their opposition to them. This was the time when politicians such as Royer-Collard and Guizot, trying to achieve a government of justice and reason, seeing the Parliament as a body which should define the interests of France rather than represent opinions, or intellectuals such as Madame de Staël and Benjamin Constant, trying to explain the significance of the French Revolution, became attached to the Charter as the salvation of the country.

But their position was necessarily weak. They could not call upon any great movement of opinion and they were dependent upon the Government and overwhelmingly on the position of the king. The fragility of their position was all the more evident since the constitution required the election of one-fifth of the Chamber annually, and the rising number of Bonapartists and ex-Revolutionaries began to cause fear and alarm. This was a movement of reaction against ultra excesses, but it could only arouse the hostility of the king and his supporters because it was essentially anti-Bourbon. The rise of these extremist groups illustrated the divisions amongst the constitutionalists. Royer-Collard and Guizot, for example, believed in the sovereignty of reason, but Benjamin Constant believed in the sovereignty of the people. There was therefore a gradual shift of political power which came to a climax in February 1820 when the Comte d'Artois's son, the Duc de Berry, who was known to be the only member of the royal family able to have children, was assassinated. It seemed that the Bourbon line might be made extinct by virtue of revolutionary action, and there was a complete change in royal policy. (In fact the Duchesse de Berry, who was pregnant at the time of the assassination, gave birth to a son.) Important Ministers such as Decazes, and influential and younger personalities such as Guizot, were dismissed. The electoral laws were revised so that the rural landowning aristocrats were given more favourable weighting as against the urban bourgeoisie. In 1821 it was a provincial nobleman, the Comte de Villèle, who became the Prime Minister. The newspapers were closely supervised; the University was put under the control of the clergy. Finally the triumph of this reaction seemed complete when on the death of Louis XVIII in September 1824 the Comte d'Artois succeeded as Charles X. He was anointed king in Reims cathedral; he announced his intentions of restoring the sacred interests of religion and of healing the last wounds of the Revolution. In practice this meant laws which would indemnify the émigrés for their loss of property during the Revolution and which would punish sacrilege with the death penalty.

It was not surprising that these policies created a reaction. When the law for giving indemnity to the émigrés came before the Chamber, it inspired a revealing debate about the Revolution. On the right it was claimed that such a law suggested that the Revolution had been legitimate and that, in fact, it was those who had acquired the lands who ought to be receiving an indemnity, since they had been duped into illegal acts. On the left it was claimed that this whole procedure was in itself illegal and, more important, that it was but a prelude to a series of other laws which would reconstitute an aristocracy and restore the Church to its old position. Thus Villèle found that he had critics everywhere. In addition there were Catholics who emphasized their Gallicanism and who found a dangerous ultramontanism in the religious ideas of the Government. The popular rumour that Charles X was a secret Jesuit gave a force to these resentments. But by the 1820s there was a new generation of electors, men who had been born after 1789 and who felt distant from the generation of the émigrés. In 1825 a funeral had provided the opportunity for the opposition which was excluded from political activity to manifest itself. General Foy's death inspired a great demonstration at his funeral and the organization of a national subscription for his children. A number of important personalities were in opposition to Villèle, Chateaubriand, for example, who had been badly treated by the Government, and Montlosier, who wrote effectively in favour of the Gallican Church. Many of the most interesting of the intellectuals were both young and associated with liberalism. Guizot (born in 1787) and Victor Cousin (born in 1792), who had lectured at the Sorbonne from 1820 to 1822; Thiers (born in 1797) who began to publish his *Histoire de la Révolution* from 1823 onwards; Charles de Rémusat (born in 1797), Jouffroy (born in 1796) and Sainte-Beuve (born in 1804) who began to publish articles in the newspaper *Le Globe*, founded in 1824. The liberals created societies and published pamphlets which not only denounced governmental manipulation of the elections, but explained how this interference could be countered. And in this atmosphere Villèle found that even the king was intriguing against him.

The elections of 1827 brought about a considerable increase in the liberal strength. Villèle found that he was outvoted by the combination of the left and right oppositions and he was replaced by a Government which had no official Prime Minister but in which the Minister of the Interior, Martignac, soon appeared as the leader. Charles X, however, regarded this as temporary and after many negotiations in August 1829 he formed a Government presided over by the Prince de Polignac, with La Bourdonnaye, who had been one of the most violent members of the Chambre Introuvable, as Minister of the Interior and General de Bourmont, who had gone over to the enemy on the eve of Waterloo, as Minister for War. The opposition newspapers denounced this Government as the Government of the Counter-Revolution, formed of Coblenz (the centre of the émigrés), Waterloo and 1815. 'On the one side,' wrote *Le Globe*, 'there is the Court, on the other side, there is the nation.' There was talk of refusing to pay taxes; there was a flurry of liberal organizations; there was talk of replacing an impossible king by his cousin, the Duc d'Orléans, and organizing a revolution similar to the English Revolution of 1688; there was a revival of republicanism and student groups got in touch with Lafayette. In March 1830 a majority of the Chamber voted an address which claimed that the views of the people were not being taken into account by the Government.

There was also an economic crisis. The harvest of 1828 had been bad and food prices had risen alarmingly. This had affected purchasing power and had probably helped to bring about a general recession of industry and trade. The banks had suffered from this recession and there was a general tendency to hold the Government responsible for all these economic difficulties. But Charles X was not prepared to give way. He was convinced that had his brother, Louis XVI, been firm and decisive, then the Revolution could have been arrested. He was convinced that he was popular, and that the opposition (which was divided) could not resist his power and authority. He believed that the expedition to conquer Algiers, which was announced in March and set sail in May, would bring a great popularity to his Government. He was confident that the support which the Church was prepared to pronounce for him, in every cathedral in the land, would render him invincible. Therefore he dissolved the Chamber and when in the election of July 1830 he still had no majority, he issued ordinances dissolving the Chamber which had never met, disqualifying many of those who had the vote, establishing a strict censorship of newspapers and periodicals, and fixing the date of new elections. The result was the *Trois Glorieuses* – 27, 28 and 29 July – in Paris. Manifestations led to the barricades going up; the king absent from Paris lost control of the situation; some of the troops fraternized with the rebels; a provisional Government was set up at the Hôtel de Ville and a vigorous campaign was organized in favour of the Duc d'Orléans. On 31 July the Duke accepted to be Lieutenant-Governor of the kingdom. On 2 August Charles X abdicated; a week later the Duke accepted the throne as Louis-Philippe I.

There are various attitudes which can be taken to the revolution of 1830. One is to suggest that there was no revolution at all. The system established in 1814 and re-established in 1815, whereby there was a monarch and two chambers (existing within a centralized administrative system) and a small wealthy electorate, persisted. It had worked regularly under Louis XVIII and Charles X until the crisis of 1830. Under Louis-Philippe it worked again. And the fact that it was Louis-Philippe emphasized the continuity. He, as Duc d'Orléans, son of the man who had been prominent in the earlier period, had received compensation from the Villèle Government in 1825, and he clearly represented the royal tradition. Nor is it true to say that there was any significant change in the personnel of those who governed France. It is true that there was a rush for new positions, and that the administration included many new faces, but there were few social implications in these changes. There were many individuals who had held public office under Napoleon. But there were no new categories of society that were suddenly brought to power and influence. In any case the revolution appeared to be essentially Parisian. The provinces had often learned of it many days after *les Trois Glorieuses*, and it could be said that the downfall of the Bourbons was as much caused by the inaction of provincial towns and the provincial nobility as by the activity of the population in Paris. This, again, is to treat the revolution of 1830 as a non-revolution, an accident of the Parisian streets which was sent to the rest of France as a sort of newsletter which required acknowledgement rather than action.

But it can be argued that the revolution of 1830 was a classical type of revolution. The ordinances appeared on Monday, 26 July, and although there were lots of people about in the streets there were few signs of excitement or interest. Yet by 29 July there had been a general movement of the population of Paris against the Government, and so many had died on the barricades that it was declared unthinkable that Charles X should rule again. Was it because there was economic crisis, because the price of food was high, because there were many unemployed? Was it because the population of Paris had been growing rapidly and there were many immigrants there who, uprooted from their normal social background, were prone to respond to crisis and unusual events with violence and aggression? It has been suggested that those most prominent in the revolution were the artisans and the skilled workers, who were responding to the fear of economic crisis and misery, and to the presence of misery, rather than to their own particular sufferings and hardships. Those who had some organization and some self-consciousness took action, and it was these factors rather than any particular economic crisis that counted. It has also been suggested that there were particular happenings, such as the hoisting of the *tricouleur* flag over the towers of Notre-Dame, that really launched the movements of enthusiasm and violence, or that it was the presence of Bonapartists with military experience that enabled the barricades to be erected successfully. All these suggestions make this revolution an important source for the understanding of all modern revolutionary movements.

It should not be forgotten that the revolution of 1830 brought about some direct changes in the organization of political life. The age for the eligibility both of the deputies and of the electorate was lowered, and the tax qualification for voting was also reduced. Thus the number of those who had the vote grew to about 166,000 and never ceased to grow during the reign of Louis-Philippe, reaching nearly a quarter of a million by 1846. The press became more resolutely free, and a form of legitimate, normal political struggle became an accepted fact.

Organized political parties were still difficult to identify, and foreign affairs tended to play an unusually large part in public life, since those who had taken part in the revolution of 1830 thought that it could be overthrown by other European powers or that it could itself be overthrown by outside intervention. But perhaps the most important significance of the revolution was to emphasize the precariousness of power in France. Just as Napoleon could be overthrown and could return, just as Louis XVIII could return and be overthrown, so Charles X had disappeared (in fact he lingered in France for an awkwardly long time before going to exile in England), and it was striking how regimes could be overthrown with no one to defend them. The realization of this was to embarrass succeeding Governments.

Another embarrassment was the whole nature of Louis-Philippe's monarchy. From the start he emphasized to the foreign powers that he was a peace-loving ruler, who did not seek to disrupt the calm of Europe in any way. Yet he felt that France's importance in the world was linked to France's association with the principle and the idea of revolution. From the start too he emphasized that he was king because he was of the blood royal, a descendant of St Louis and a Bourbon. Yet he knew that he was king because of revolution. It could have been a revolution which, without his opportune arrival on the scene, would have led to a republic, so that it was, as Victor Hugo called it, a turned-in revolution ('une révolution rentrée') or a confiscated revolution. But it was a revolution none the less and although Louis-Philippe's insistence caused him to be recognized eventually by all the sovereigns of Europe as one of them, yet he remained a monarch whose position was ambiguous.

The revolutionary tradition was maintained right from the beginning of the reign. There was always the possibility of counter-revolution, of those who believed in the Bourbons taking action. They were particularly strong amongst the nobility, in Brittany and in the south. Worried prefects reported that there were whole regions where aristocrats, owning large areas of land, sometimes in isolated and backward parts of the country, maintained loyalty to the Bourbon family. In the west there was the tradition of Vendée and the Counter-Revolution; in the south, especially where there were Protestants, there was the tradition of the White Terror. In both regions the Church was opposed to the new regime and in 1832 the Duchesse de Berry tried to raise these two areas. There was also the possibility of social revolution. Those who were disappointed at the betrayal of the people's cause, since the people had risen in Paris and had fought and died on the barricades, organized themselves into clubs for the furtherance of revolution. In foreign countries such as Belgium and Poland they identified and supported the cause of freedom. For others, it was through assassinating Louis-Philippe that the needed changes would come, and that monarch's life was frequently in danger.

Yet revolution was not immediately successful. There were legitimist plots, scares, sulks and manifestations, but there was no legitimist uprising. It was as if the legitimist sentiments of the aristocracy and the clergy were not strong enough to force a real rupture with the bourgeoisie or to destroy their co-operation in business and officialdom. There was also the parade of socialism, and there were demonstrations of popular violence. Yet such movements were invariably linked to particular grievances, and once these were settled it was hard to see the workers as a real revolutionary force. It was all typified by the episode of Louis-Napoleon. Napoleon having died in 1820 and his son in 1830, it was his nephew who became the pretender to the imperial crown, and he attempted to seize power more than once. Under Louis-Philippe these attempts were fiascos, but his very presence and the fact that people were prepared to fear his success were examples of how power was fundamentally weak, although in practice convinced and resolute. It was as if power was always there for the taking. The unique position of Paris in the centralized administrative system meant that France was particularly vulnerable to revolution.

The men who ruled France after 1830 were all anti-revolutionary, although connected with the moderate and legal revolution which had been accomplished by the Third Estate. Louis-Philippe, the son of Philippe-Égalité, had fought at Valmy and Jemappes; Guizot, a Protestant, had a father who had been associated with the ideas of 1789 and with the Girondins; the Duc de Broglie was married to the daughter of Madame de Staël; the fathers of all three of them had been guillotined. Casimir Périer, the banker, was the son of Claude Périer who had led the revolt of the Estates in Dauphiné; Thiers had a father who had been ruined during the Revolution; Soult, Gérard, Mortier, Molé and others had all served under Napoleon. It was clear that there would be no going back to the principles of the *ancien régime* and this issue was definitively closed. On the other hand, beyond this restricted governmental personnel, there were those who believed that the revolution should go forward, and new generations and different social groups looked to further developments. One of the difficulties was that there was no agreed procedure whereby the system could either be stabilized or reformed. Parliament had worked reasonably well under the Restoration and a political tradition was growing up. But no political parties or organizations had taken shape. There had been groups that had been associated with particular ideas or with particular individuals, and it had been possible to speak in general terms about 'ultras' or about 'liberals', but there was no party organization as there were no traditional political parties. When men were elected to the Chamber it was often not known whether they would vote for the Government or against it, since it was customary in elections for candidates to make profession of their independence. Undoubtedly the fundamental reason for the failure of political parties to develop was that, although the electorate was a very small one, it was socially and ideologically very varied. In 1831 the revised Charter increased the number of electors to more than 160,000, and the normal process whereby wealth grew caused more men to qualify as electors, so that by 1846 there were nearly 250,000. But whereas in Paris there was a large number of electors and an election represented a struggle between political tendencies and an argument between ideas as well as interests, in some departments the elections concerned only a few hundred electors and hardly represented a political issue. It was an affair of local personalities, or of local matters, in which the prefect or sub-prefect could play an important role, as could all the notabilities of birth, wealth or profession. It was clearly impossible for such deputies to be welded into any national system of organized ideas and interests.

This incoherence of the Chamber of Deputies helped to create other forms of political instability. The Chamber of Deputies never lasted the full five years for which it had been elected. Apart from the partial elections held in October 1830 to fill vacancies, many of which had been caused by the revolution, there were six general elections held in less than eighteen years. More remarkable still was the ministerial instability of the first ten years of the reign. Up to October 1840 there were fifteen different Governments, some lasting for a few days only. After October 1840 there was virtually only the one Government, dominated by Guizot. It is clear that personal elements were important in creating these ministerial changes, and the fact that there was no obvious reason why one man should be Prime Minister rather than another must have exacerbated personal rivalries. But there were two other factors which helped to shape the nature of political life. There was the question of the monarch. What was the role of the king under the Charter? Since Louis-Philippe was king because he was of the blood royal it could be argued that his political role was fundamental and that he should be the dominant influence in government. But since he was also king as the result of revolution, and since the Charter was the basis of all political action, then it could also be argued that the royal role should be less decisive than that of the Ministers and legislators. In the circumstances Louis-Philippe was always determined to be an active and powerful king, but he preferred to act by stealth rather than by royal command, and it was clearly in his interests to be a permanent presence amongst the shifting, uncertain and shapeless political forces. Thus this astute political king contributed to the instability of the system.

There was also the question of foreign affairs. The July Monarchy was particularly conscious of the importance of what went on in neighbouring countries because it seemed that its whole destiny depended upon it. The revolution was a change in the Vienna settlement of 1815, and it was always possible that the other powers of Europe would intervene in order to restore the rightful royal family and to crush a dangerous revolution in its birthplace. Louis-Philippe was quick to send special emissaries to the important capitals of Europe in order to reassure his fellow monarchs and he was always anxious to present himself as a lover of peace and order. But July 1830 in Paris was not an isolated European revolution. The risings in Brussels and Warsaw were confirmation of the fact that revolution was a more general phenomenon, and there were those who believed that it was the opportunity for France to put herself at the head of a European movement. In this way the cause of liberty would be sustained, French power and influence would be increased and the humiliations of 1815 would be erased. There was another calculation. Just as the revolution had been impelled forward by the war of 1792, so the French involvement in the national movements of the 1830s would bring about further political and social changes within France. This calculation became more important when after 1834 there was a falling-off in the intensity of social movements. It seemed that the only way in which any form of domestic change could be accomplished would be by some involvement in foreign war. And even those who did not wish for considerable change at home thought that a successful war would consolidate the throne and believed that it was only in patriotism that a divided nation could find its unity. Thus the conduct of foreign affairs achieved an unusual importance and different views of what the Government should do helped to increase the instability of Governments and the complications of politics.

Yet France did not become involved in European war. In 1830 and 1831 Louis-Philippe rejected the opportunity of occupying Belgium or of seeing one of his sons become king of the Belgians. In 1836 he refused to allow Thiers to patronize an armed intervention in Spanish affairs. In 1840 when France had found herself diplomatically isolated because Mehemet Ali, the Pasha of Egypt and the ally of France, was threatening to attack the Ottoman Empire, he again dismissed Thiers rather than allow the affairs of the Middle East to involve him in a war on the Rhine and in the Alps. Only in Algeria was there constant warfare as the Government decided to maintain this last conquest of the Bourbons and found themselves obliged to extend their occupation to cover the whole coast-line and much of the interior. Just as there were many who criticized Louis-Philippe and his Ministers for their alleged timidity in Europe, so there were those who were quick to point to the expenditure of men and money in order to hold on to a territory that appeared to have little value and few possibilities.

Yet all this political discussion, or the debate on foreign affairs, concerned only a relatively few people. It was true that there were moments of excitement, as in 1840, when certain issues appeared to be of vital importance, and Paris was the scene of endless debate and discussion. But there was a vital difference between the small number of those who had political rights (the *pays légal*) and the very large number that could neither vote nor become a deputy (the *pays réel*). Newspapers were important, and the number of regular readers increased (especially after the foundation of *La Presse* in 1836, a cheap newspaper which carried many advertisements and serialized novels), but they only reached a small minority of the population. This was a moment too when the publication of certain books had a remarkable impact upon the public, and when literature and politics were closely allied, yet even writers such as Hugo or Lamartine cannot be thought of as reaching the masses of the population. News-sheets, popular songs (especially those written by Béranger), almanacs, printed illustrations and various sorts of devotional works must have reached a much wider public and inculcated it with stories of famous crimes, a constant anti-clericalism, a nostalgia for Napoleon and a belief in miracles.

The population as a whole was most concerned with three areas of activity. One was local government, especially municipal government since the law of 1831 gave the right to elect a municipal council to more than a million Frenchmen. These councils had a relatively restricted importance since it was the Government that nominated (and could dismiss) the mayors, and the centralized administrative system gave little opportunity for municipalities to influence their decisions. But local politics could arouse excitements and it could create a consciousness of political issues that was important for the future.

A second subject of activity and interest (and one which directly affected municipal government) was education. In 1833 Guizot, as Minister for Public Instruction, passed his law on primary education. This stated that every commune was obliged to have a school and a school-teacher, whilst every department would eventually have an institution for training teachers (an *École Normale*). Education was neither made free nor compulsory, although it was theoretically possible for the children of the indigent poor to go to school without paying. The municipal authorities, who were responsible for the supervision of the school, were sometimes hostile to the idea of education, and parents could often see no reason why their children should learn to read and write. But the number of those who attended school began to rise, the number of those that could neither read nor write began to decline. Within the villages the presence of a schoolmaster (the *instituteur*) and his relations with the priest was often the subject of controversy and invariably the source of debate and discussion. This debate was not as acrimonious nor as considerable as the debate on secondary education which brought about a confrontation between 'the sons of Saint-Louis and the sons of Voltaire', in which the Catholics claimed the right to send their children to secondary schools, run by those that they knew to be Catholics, and the supporters of the existing system believed that the maintenance of some sort of State control over secondary schools and teachers was essential to the unity of France. But it meant that there was a strong movement of opinion amongst Catholics, stretching over classes, that there was no reason why they should support the regime, whilst *instituteurs* in their conflicts with the priest and the municipal authorities wanted to see a Government which would help them more decisively.

The third activity which concerned the mass of the population was obviously their work. Under the July Monarchy the progress of industrialization continued and there was also a necessary progress in agriculture to keep pace with the steady rise of the population. More land was cultivated, new crops were introduced and the peasantry as a whole profited from the remarkable progress in communications (canals, roads, railways) which was the most dramatic economic change of the period. Thus the statistical record in both industrial and agricultural production was favourable, but within this general picture there were important items of hardship and crisis. Thus, in agricultural terms, there were conflicts in the countryside as the wealthy landowners and peasants tried to take over common land, as the administration tried to plant trees, as the development of towns brought about a decline of rural industry, as the small peasantry determinedly tried to acquire more land and ran into debt, as a large population meant an unsafe dependence upon food harvests. In industrial terms there remained the three types of workers, the artisans (who were by far the most numerous), the factory workers (usually in a few towns) and the domestic workers either in the countryside or the towns. As always their conditions varied, living conditions in Paris or in Lille, for example, being worse than in Alsace or in the south where the progress of industrialization was much slower and where the workers' links with the countryside remained much more meaningful. But since industrial production of all sorts tended to be closely tied to the market, there was an insecurity in the life of all workers. There were always those that were unemployed, and their numbers could rise alarmingly given any form of economic crisis. If these working populations appear to have faced the prospect of a life of terrible hardship and the possibility of an early death (since the working-class areas of some towns were known to have a much higher mortality rate than the areas inhabited by the more comfortably off) with a certain fatalism, they could not but be conscious of the nature of the economic situation and the terms of their employment.

Between the peasantry and the workers, and the controlling political élites, there lay a number of social categories. There were doctors, lawyers, veterinary surgeons, journalists, schoolteachers and students; there were all sorts of officials or *fonctionnaires*; there were shopkeepers, artisans (such as coopers or smiths), merchants, café proprietors and many others. These were to be distinguished from the working population often because they had access to wealth, because they had power through their functions or because they had been educated, but they could often have been only recently removed from these working classes. They were sufficiently near to them to know their bad conditions, and whether through sympathy or through fear, they believed that the Government should do something about them. They were usually excluded from political power. Sometimes, as with the financing of railway construction, the wealthier amongst them, in the provinces for example, found themselves excluded from the opportunities of investment. For all of them the development of financial concentration, the increasing importance of mechanization, the need for higher standards of education than hitherto, meant that social mobility was becoming more difficult. All the indications show that whilst in an expanding economy there were always new opportunities being created, it was increasingly necessary to have some sort of capital to begin with.

Thus a firm impression is created that in the July Monarchy there was a small élite that had achieved the monopoly of all power, whether economic or political, and that beyond it lay the great mass of the population, in which a middle bourgeoisie was forcibly allied with peasants and workers since they were all excluded from power. This suggestion that there was such a polarization of social groups was made by Marx, and by certain of his contemporaries. It has to be modified in many ways. Many of the political élite were the old political élite, that is to say the landowners often noble or having pretensions to nobility, who still dominated the electoral circumscriptions. In 1840 137 deputies out of 459 gave their profession simply as 'landowner' (without any other profession being mentioned, although most of them must have had other interests). The administrative and official class remained vitally important and had its own professional interests and cohesion. The wealth of France remained remarkably scattered throughout the country and it is simply not true to say that it was being seized by a relatively small number of men. But under the July Monarchy it seemed as if the process whereby the government of the country would come into the hands of such an élite had begun. In a country where suspicion and exaggeration were part of the political tradition, it was not surprising that it was widely believed that government was conducted in the interests of a small group of men. It was not only Stendhal who, travelling between Dol-de-Bretagne and Saint-Malo, felt depressed as he encountered the rich bourgeois of the July Monarchy triumphant. Exclusion could take place on many levels and as one famous deputy, Alphonse de Lamartine, saw himself always excluded from office, in 1843 he entered the opposition 'pour toujours'. But for him, this was the opposition to the whole system. Like those who had remained loyal to the Bourbons, or like those who dreamed of a Jacobin republic, he did not want to reform the system but to change it. 'Guizot, Thiers, Molé, Passy, Dufaure,' he said, naming the most prominent members of the political spectrum. 'Five ways of saying the same thing.' Thus the system of the July Monarchy had its enemies both within and without.

In the summer of 1846 the Government, which was presided over by Marshal Soult, but which was effectively directed by Guizot, won a considerable electoral victory. It had been in power since October 1840 and Guizot felt entitled to boast that France had the most stable Government in Europe. Perhaps it was this victory that began the crisis. It seemed as if the Government was immovable, that it was permanently blocking the way to change and progress, that the 'outs' were always to be 'out'. The moderate opposition decided to press for parliamentary and electoral reform as a means of dislodging the Government; allegations that the Government had won its majority by means of corruption became frequent (and they were usually exaggerated); those whose attitude towards power had always been more violent were confirmed in their view that it would only be by some violent shock that they would get rid of the existing regime.

But the real crisis was economic, and it took place in various phases. The first was traditional, that is to say that it began with a bad harvest in 1846, leading to exceptionally high prices for bread in the spring of 1847. It must be noted, however, that it did not affect the whole of France, that in certain places it was caused as much by fear as by an actual shortage, and that it did not last long. Well before the harvest of 1847, food prices were falling. The second was an industrial crisis and was less traditional. To some extent the high price of food affected purchasing power and thereby caused industrial production to be reduced, but essentially the crisis was one of credit and it had preceded the bad harvest of 1846. The economic developments of the 1840s, particularly the construction of railways, had absorbed vast quantities of capital. Suddenly it appeared that there was no capital available, and that the intense activity of 1845 had overstrained the resources of the money market. The railway promoters found that they had underestimated their costs, many businesses and enterprises became particularly conscious of the strains of progress. Throughout 1847 there was a shortage of credit and a consequent slump in business activity. The third phase of the economic crisis coincided with this slump and it was based upon the fear that the Government would be unable to meet its financial obligations. The State had greatly increased its commitments (over education, communications and Algeria, for example) and yet it existed on a small budget with the manipulation of various funds and with a policy of loans. All this led to some alarmist comments which weakened the Government's position. Once again, the extent of these crises should not be exaggerated. There were areas and industries which did not suffer from a regression; there were those who were claiming that the worst of the crisis was over by the end of 1847; many were reassured by the Minister of Finance who said that the Government would be able to meet its obligations.

But the situation was gloomy. The agricultural crisis had led to various movements in the countryside, markets had sometimes been pillaged and the movement of grain had been interfered with. The recession had led to a high rate of unemployment, particularly in coal-mining, textile production and railway construction. The money market was jumpy and was anxious about any form of political crisis, so that the Government felt unable to take any initiative and its majority began to drift away. Opinion was affected too by foreign affairs and by a number of domestic scandals. Both Louis-Philippe and Guizot had always wanted to have a special understanding with England, but this was broken in 1846 when the British Government reacted strongly to the son of the French king marrying a Spanish princess and creating the possibility of a French succession to the Spanish throne, so that it was said that the British alliance had been sacrificed to purely dynastic interests. Subsequently Guizot collaborated with Metternich and with the Continental powers, a collaboration which was not only unpopular but which was also unsuccessful (their support for the Swiss Catholics, for example, did not prevent them from being defeated). Even the final defeat of the Algerian nationalist leader, Abd-el-Kader, in 1847, gave rise to bitter dispute since it was claimed that the king's son, the Duc d'Aumale, had mishandled the terms of surrender. At home it was revealed that former Ministers had been guilty of corruption; a prominent member of the Chamber of Peers murdered his wife and then committed suicide (it was widely rumoured that he had been allowed to escape); a minor scandal concerning the Government's use of patronage affected one of Guizot's closest collaborators and therefore was said to implicate even him.

Naturally none of this created a revolutionary situation. If the widespread discontent with the Government and the general pessimism about the situation can be analysed in terms of long-standing grievances, and if one can point out that the easy violence with which orators such as Lamartine had been speaking about revolution was bound to have had some effect, it remains true that the events of

February 1848 were largely accidental. A demonstration organized against the Government's refusal to allow a reform banquet to be held in Paris convinced the king that he should dismiss Guizot, which he did on 23 February. Later that evening troops fired on the crowds in a moment of panic and fifty-two people were killed. Some of these corpses were piled on to a cart which was taken on a torch-lit procession of the city. This inflamed the population which put up more barricades; columns of troops had to be withdrawn; a small resolute group of republicans demanded the proclamation of the republic and began to circulate the names of a provisional Government. Finally, just after noon on 24 February, Louis-Philippe, by now elderly and apprehensive, abdicated in favour of his nine-year-old grandson. But the crowds invaded the Chamber of Deputies, all the members of the royal family fled or went into hiding, and a Government was chosen by insurgents and groups of republicans.

Thus after a few confused hours the July Monarchy had been brought down. As in 1830, the rest of France was faced by a Parisian *fait accompli* and there was no movement anywhere to support the disappearing dynasty. But there were important differences between 1830 and 1848. In 1848 all organized and official power disappeared. The royal family had gone and there was no younger branch which could take over; the Chambers had been dispersed; no one was prepared to uphold the Charter; the provisional Government of eleven men included eight who had been republicans at a time when it is thought that there were less than 5,000 republicans in Paris. And very rapidly the demands of the revolutionary crowds made themselves felt. On the morning of 25 February armed workmen interrupted the deliberations of the new Government and demanded that the right to work should be guaranteed. In consequence such a decree was drawn up, the National Workshops were eventually created and a Special Commission for workers was set up to look after the interests of working men and to foster their organizations. The impression was created that the revolution of 1848 was a revolution which sought to make life better for all the population. It was a revolution which looked back to the days of hope in the great Revolution, which it still saw as a model, but it also looked forward to a future of change. It was believed that things would never be the same again. 1848 was socialist, romantic, utopian, and even where this created more apprehension than enthusiasm, the revolution was accepted everywhere, supporters both of the Bourbons and of Louis-Philippe declared that they were republicans, priests blessed the trees of liberty which were planted throughout the country, bourgeois and *notables* of all sorts fraternized with the workers in great demonstrations. Exactly one week after Louis-Philippe's abdication the provisional Government declared that universal manhood suffrage existed in France, a form of voting which few had believed in and which existed nowhere else in Europe. When the elections took place in April, something like 97 per cent of those who voted had never voted before and the electorate leapt from 250,000 to 9,000,000. In a fever of discussion, it seemed that France was undergoing a rapid and complete revolution.

But the election revealed that the clubs and the newspapers of Paris were not representative of the whole of France. There was a general rejection of those who had ruled under the July Monarchy (Thiers, for example, was defeated) but the majority of the Assembly should be classed as moderate, drawn mainly from the provincial bourgeoisie, including more than seventy nobles and not a single peasant. Probably most of the Chamber had been monarchists before 1848 (including a fair number of Legitimists). In some parts of France there were worker demonstrations in protest against these results and there was a serious demonstration in Paris on 15 May when the Assembly eliminated the socialist Left from the provisional Government. People such as Barbès, Blanqui and Raspail, who were appearing as the leaders of the extremist groups in Paris, were imprisoned, and both Marx and Tocqueville described the situation as being one of class warfare. Once again it was the artisans in the traditional crafts and the recent immigrants into Paris who were providing the shock troops for the expected, final showdown, and once again it was in conditions of considerable economic distress that the insurrection took place. When the Government decided to send men from the National Workshops into the provinces, organized groups of workmen protested on 22 June. Believing that the Republic was in danger, that the rising was socialist and was aimed at the destruction of property and that rival political groups (including Legitimists, Orleanists and Bonapartists) were fomenting insurrection, the Government decided on a brutal repression. The army and the National Guard, both from Paris and the provinces, killed some thousands of the insurgents and more than 11,000 were imprisoned.

From June onwards the Government, under General Cavaignac who had been the man primarily responsible for the repression, attempted to consolidate the existing institutions and introduced a number of moderate reforms. But its main preoccupation was with drawing up a new constitution. The most notable feature of this constitution was that the executive was to consist of a President elected for four years by universal manhood suffrage. It was true that this President had many checks on his power, and a single Chamber, also elected by universal male suffrage, was given the exclusive right to make the laws and to decide upon war and peace. But the position of the President was clearly to be vital to the constitution and there were many republicans who had doubts about the wisdom of giving such power to one man, and who wondered whether such a President were compatible with the principle of the Republic. But a powerful speech by Lamartine in favour of direct popular sovereignty won the day and it was arranged that there would be a presidential election in December 1848.

A number of candidates were announced well in advance of this date. The last was that of Louis-Napoleon Bonaparte, the nephew of the emperor. He had not been well known before 1848 and he had not returned to France from his English exile until September. But he had been elected in by-elections by a number of different departments as well as in Paris and he had entered into negotiations with the different political groups that used to meet in the Rue de Poitiers, where Legitimists, Orleanists (including Thiers) and Catholics had weekly discussions. Partly because they had no agreed candidate of their own, partly because it seemed that the name of Bonaparte was being successful, and possibly because they thought they could dominate a man who seemed inexperienced and unimpressive, they decided to support him. Louis-Napoleon was elected by almost 75 per cent of those that voted.

The Second Republic and the Second Empire

It is not as easy as some historians have thought to explain Louis-Napoleon's success. It is not enough to suggest that it was simply his name that served him ('his candidature dates from Austerlitz,' Victor Hugo had remarked when he had first been mentioned as a possible deputy). Nor is it enough to suggest that since the first need of a saviour of society is to have something to save society from, it was the fear of further social movements and insurrections that incited people to vote for him. In spite of the understanding between Thiers and Louis-Napoleon many of the notables, some of the bishops and conservative newspapers supported Cavaignac who always presented himself as a man of order. Nor can one say that Louis-Napoleon was elected by the peasantry, and that the election was the 'coup d'état of the peasants' as

Marx put it. His votes were consistently in the majority in most of the large towns. One is therefore forced to the conclusion that Louis-Napoleon won votes from all sections of the population, partly because of the ambiguity of his position, since few people knew him and since he encouraged everyone to expect things from; him and partly because to vote for him was to protest against all the things that had gone before, whether it was economic distress, disorder, the conservatism of the republican Government, Catholic discontent with the educational system, the continued supremacy of the *notables* or the feelings of uncertainty which had both preceded and followed February 1848. It was as if it were Louis-Napoleon who divided Frenchmen the least. His situation was strong, but part of his strength lay in the very ambiguity that surrounded him, and he was to remain a puzzling and unpredictable ruler. His situation was also weak since he did not know France, he had no experience of Government, he had no organized political support and his constitutional powers were surrounded by complicated restrictions.

He was known as the Prince-President and he began his functions by showing considerable political skill. The press was subsidized, different parts of the country were visited, the Catholics were pleased by being allowed to establish primary and secondary schools, conservatives were impressed by his dismantling of radical organizations. The sending of a French army to Rome to destroy the recently created Roman Republic and to restore papal authority was satisfying to Catholic opinion and was an assertion of the importance of France in the world. But Napoleon had also to appear as the hero of the liberals and democrats. He did this by criticizing Pope Pius IX, who was following a policy of reaction, and by saying that he had not sent an army to Rome to stifle Italian liberty. But above all he was enabled to do this by the action of the Assembly (dated in 1849) which sought to remove the vote from some three million Frenchmen; he appeared as the opponent of these reactionaries and frequently pointed to his own position as the representative of the people. Thus when on 2 December 1851 a carefully planned and neatly executed *coup d'état* arrested the leaders of the opposition and dissolved the Assembly it was possible for this to be presented as a democratic measure. It was announced that universal suffrage was restored and that the people would be asked to accept or reject what had happened by plebiscite. There were armed movements against this, especially in the south, and the repression involved the imprisonment of some 30,000. In Paris 80,000 troops were deployed against a few hundred workers (although a contemporary observer spoke of 2,000 insurgents being killed). But the plebiscite gave an overwhelming approval to Louis-Napoleon's overthrow of the Assembly. On 2 December 1852, the anniversary of the *coup d'état* (2 December was also the anniversary of Austerlitz), Louis-Napoleon made his formal entry into Paris as the Emperor Napoleon III.

It was strange that Napoleon III was so frequently to cast himself as the successor to his uncle, to revive the imperial emblems, to make 15 August (Napoleon's birthday) a national festival, even to consider bringing the Pope to Paris in order to crown him. Napoleon III was very unlike Napoleon I. Whilst his ancestor had been decisive, energetic, talkative and daring, Napoleon III was uncertain, lazy, silent and cautious. Napoleon I was a gambler; Napoleon III tried to keep all his options open for as long as possible. Napoleon I was a soldier; Napoleon III was more of an intellectual, a connoisseur of ideas. But where they did resemble each other was in a shrewd and cynical detachment, which caused them both to realize that there were different elements in Bonapartism and which led them to try and keep the initiative, always to be one step in advance of their opponents. Napoleon III tried to show that he was both an authoritarian ruler and a liberal, that he was a defender of property and a friend of the worker, that he believed in peace but that France could embark on an adventurous policy abroad. In political terms the 1850s were characterized by the emperor's control of executive and legislative power, with the Senate nominated by him, a Legislative Assembly which could not initiate legislation and which was packed by governmental interference, with a press and a theatre that were strictly controlled, and an administration that had extensive police powers. All political opposition seemed to have disappeared and the official opposition in the Legislative Assembly could be counted on the fingers of one hand.

But this personal supremacy was never so evident as in the series of measures by which the emperor decided to liberalize his regime. In 1859 there was an amnesty; in 1860 both the Senate and the Legislative Assembly were given the right to frame, discuss and vote an annual address; in 1861 the right was given to the press to publish the debates; in 1863 a Minister was given the function of defending Government policy in the Assembly; 1867 and 1868 saw the Chamber given the right to ask Ministers questions, newspapers benefited from a slight relaxation of their control and public meetings became easier to organize.

The result of all these reforms was that in the elections of 1863 and 1869 the opposition grew considerably. But Napoleon III regarded this as an incentive to further change. In September 1869 the Chambers were given more freedom over their own affairs and control over business. The move towards a form of parliamentary government reached completion when in January 1870 Émile Ollivier was invited to lead the Government and to regard himself as the leader of a parliamentary majority. But in May 1870 the emperor revealed the complexity of his thought by submitting his reforms to a plebiscite. More than 80 per cent of those who had voted approved, so that it was as if the Empire had been founded for the second time. Two powers existed: the power of the emperor, approved by the population as a whole, and the power of the Assembly and of the Chief Minister. It was a curious situation.

Doubtless none of this political evolution would have been possible without two other features of the Second Empire. The one was that this was an era of business confidence and industrial prosperity. There was considerable industrial growth, mechanization spread, railway construction was important, Paris was replanned and there was a large extension in the credit facilities available (as in the amount of capital exported). In 1860 an economic agreement with England reduced the amount of protection available for French industries and this caused some firms to reduce the number of workers employed or to try to reduce their wages. It also aroused much discontent amongst the employers. From this time onwards Napoleon found himself opposed and criticized both by the employers and by the workers. His attempts to create some sort of labour legislation for the latter seemed inadequate to the workers, whilst they appeared to be a betrayal to those who were employers. The other feature of the Second Empire was its active foreign policy. In 1854 Napoleon associated himself with the British in the Near East, and fought in the Crimean war with Britain and Turkey. The peace conference at the end of this war was held in Paris in 1856, and Napoleon was sometimes called 'the emperor of Europe'. In 1859 he made war on Austria in support of Italian unification, but after some victories he suddenly deserted his ally and made peace (it was then that Nice and Savoy were annexed to France). He intervened in Indo-China (making Cochin-China a colony and Cambodia a protectorate), Syria, Mexico and West Africa. But every one of his successes was double-edged, as other powers were both impressed and suspicious of this activity. At home the Catholics resented his support for the nationalists, liberals regretted that he had not gone further, and the conservative-minded wondered about the wisdom of these adventures.

There are those who have claimed that there was an inevitability about the decline of the Second Empire. From the 1850s onwards, it is suggested that the emperor was simply alienating one element of French opinion after another. Bonapartism was meant to be a consensus, a bringing-together of different parts of society; since it was no longer doing this then it was no longer fulfilling its function, and however much the emperor tried to share his authority, there was no getting away from failure. Yet it is difficult to accept this point of view. As has been shown here, there was always a deliberate ambiguity in Napoleon's position and there is no evidence that he was forced into making concessions. He showed his force by retaining the initiative, and there was a general agreement that the liberal Empire of 1870 was a strong regime. Some of the opposition had been won over, however reluctantly, and the remaining opposition was discouraged. It was true that the emperor was no longer in good health and that he had lost much of his vigour. The empress (Eugénie de Montijo, who had become empress in 1853 and who gave birth to a male heir in 1856) was critical of the reforms, and the court was a great centre of intrigue. In January 1871 Prince Pierre Bonaparte had shot a journalist, Victor Noir, this giving rise to a ferociously hostile outcry. But when war eventually came, the opponents of the Government were saddened because they thought that it would strengthen the Empire. No one saw it as a means of facilitating the destruction of a doomed regime.

The belief that the succession of a Hohenzollern to the Spanish throne was a form of Prussian encirclement of France was a curious exaggeration, and the French insistence that the Prussian king should renounce in perpetuity any Hohenzollern claim to the Spanish throne was a petulant foolishness. From this came the impression that both the French and the Germans had been insulted and Napoleon responded to the excitement by declaring war in July 1870. He was to find that France was diplomatically isolated; that earlier military reforms were incomplete since they had come up against so much opposition; that the officers in charge were incompetent, often having been chosen for reasons of favouritism or political preference. The emperor himself put the seal on a confused mobilization by himself taking command when he was physically unable to do so. The result was that with one French army encircled at Metz, the emperor was forced to surrender at Sedan on 2 September 1870. The principal part of the constitution was thus removed. The Prince Impérial was too young and no one had any confidence in the empress. Fearful of a more radical riposte, since the war continued and since the road to Paris lay open, a group of moderate republicans proclaimed the Republic on 4 September 1870.

The Third Republic to 1914

There was nothing new in a French regime collapsing and in there being no support for it. But the situation in 1870 was spectacular in its uncertainty. The Republic had been proclaimed. But the republicans were conscious of the fact that they were a minority in the country; they were divided amongst themselves, since a new generation had grown up, which had little in common with the persistent utopianism of the 1848 generation, and since there was a great variety of opinions sheltering under the name of republican, stretching from a simple resentment of Napoleon III to more ambitious plans for a social and democratic organization; the differences amongst republicans were also regional. In these circumstances how could a group of inexperienced men hope to face up to the crisis of a continued German advance and the absence of any settled Government? For the war, they prepared themselves for a long siege in Paris, and a prominent young republican, Gambetta, left Paris by balloon in order to raise troops and to direct provisional Governments, first at Tours, then at Bordeaux. So far as the settling of the institutions of the country was concerned, they were not agreed. There were those republicans who claimed that the Republic existed and that no one could abolish it, even by virtue of universal suffrage (here there was the fear that the peasantry, the majority of the population, would continue to vote Bonapartist, so that the republicans saw themselves in opposition to the *campagnocratie*). But other republicans thought that it was necessary to consult the population. There were many moderates who felt that the situation was disturbing: within a besieged Paris the attempts at breaking out had been accompanied by flurries of social movements, and on the Loire Gambetta's raising of armies had also given rise to a violent patriotism which promised to be uncontrollable. There seemed to be a connection between continuing the war and accepting forms of political radicalism which would destroy the social organization of the country. It was in these circumstances that the opinion of the moderates prevailed and with German consent to an armistice elections were held in February. The circumstances of the electoral campaign were strikingly unusual, and perhaps too much should not be made of the fact that an overwhelmingly large majority of the country voted conservative and monarchist, that is to say, voted for peace. There had never been an elected assembly that had had so many aristocrats. The supporters of Gambetta were a mere handful. In the light of this result the Government was able to ask for peace terms, and at the beginning of March preliminary terms were drawn up by which the Germans annexed all of Alsace and part of Lorraine, whilst imposing a heavy indemnity and the right to occupy certain areas. It was to the elder statesman Thiers that the Assembly had turned and who seemed to represent the hope of returning to a more stable situation.

But not everyone was in full agreement with this policy. In Paris particularly, after a long siege, it seemed that the Government had not done everything which was necessary to protect it. When the Government decided to leave Bordeaux and to return, not to Paris, but to Versailles, it seemed that an unpatriotic Government was seeking to downgrade the city. When the Government decided to disband the National Guard, thus ending the only regular wage which many Parisians had, and to render all Parisians liable to pay bills and debts again (a liability which had been suspended during the siege), then it seemed that there was being made a deliberate attack on Parisians. Consequently when the Government attempted to remove cannon from Montmartre on the night of 17–18 March 1871, there was an insurrection, probably caused by a mixture of panic as well as resentment. It was true that this accident became graver as the crowds killed two generals, but the real gravity developed as the rising began to appear in the perspective of a wider meaning. The Paris insurrectionaries were patriots, fighting against the Government in Versailles and the provincial bourgeoisie, just as an earlier revolutionary Government had fought against the court and the provinces. Thiers, perhaps profiting from his experience of 1830 and 1848, withdrew all his forces from the capital, and the insurrectionaries found themselves in charge of the city. They therefore organized elections and in April a municipal Government, the Commune, was set up. In France there were therefore two Governments.

The Paris Commune of 1871 is a complicated subject. It has rightly been said that it is one of those incidents where the legend is more vital than the fact. One of the legends was that Paris fell under the rule of a mob, in which foreigners were prominent, and that this mob, putting forward the heady and dangerous principles of socialism, mixed with atheism, immorality and drunkenness, held the population in terror. Hence, in expiation, the Basilica of the Sacré Cœur was subsequently built at Montmartre. The other legend was that the rising of the Commune was the first worker rising in world history, and that it was here that the practice of a Marxist socialism was tried Consequently there has been a cult of the *communards*, especially in revolutionary or left-wing political parties. Modern historians tend to be more sympathetic to the second view than to the first, but tend to emphasize certain features. As with all French revolutions there are different perspectives through which the Commune can be viewed. It is true that from the 1860s onwards there was an increase in worker organizations. The emperor himself had helped to sponsor co-operative and mutual credit societies, but under the influence of Proudhon's ideas, there were organizations which sought to further worker power and to reduce government centralization. Amongst the new radical organizations too there was a demand for endowing Paris with municipal liberties, such as the right to elect a mayor. During the war and the siege, the people of Paris had found themselves in an unusual position. They had suffered great hardships and they had been extensively organized in order to fight, as they saw it, for the defence of the nation and of the Republic. They were suspicious of being betrayed, whether by officers or by politicians. Perhaps they had become accustomed to violence: at all events the attempt to remove the cannon from Montmartre appeared as an assault upon them and when they set up a rival Government then they had committed themselves. Thiers and the Versailles Government did not attempt to negotiate. Within this impasse, and in an atmosphere of freedom and exaltation, the leaders of Paris began to discuss the future. They had plans for the establishment of liberty, the organization of the municipalities of France, the spread of education and the emancipation of the proletariat. There was a great variety of ideas, but obviously those who were familiar with socialist or Marxist doctrines expressed themselves most forcibly, and attacks on the Church and on those who exploited their workers became frequent. A number of the ideas put forward, such as that for the emancipation of women, were very advanced, and the persistence of such discussions suggests that many of the *communards* were conscious of the uniqueness of their position. Meanwhile Paris was governed in a moderate, efficient way (one English commentator noted that the streets of Paris were kept clean) and whilst the Commune adopted some socialist or semi-socialist measures, such as fixing minimum wages in a number of workshops, and exploring the possibility of reopening abandoned workshops under worker co-operatives, it was in practice timid and cautious.

In the organization of its own defence it was also ineffective. In 1871 the troops of the Versailles Government stormed and took the city. In the final week of May (21–28 May) there was an onslaught on the forces of the Commune which far outdid the repression of June 1848. Perhaps 20,000 were killed in the fighting, some 50,000 were arrested and there were many thousands who fled. Since the *communards* had largely been men from the artisan and working class, this meant that the working population of Paris was decimated. The Versailles Government was triumphant and secure, and when partial elections were held in July 1871 in order to fill a large number of seats (143) which were vacant because a deputy could be elected to more than one circumscription, the republicans were overwhelmingly successful.

Thus within a relatively short time there had been a number of political experiences in France. France had voted imperialist, then monarchist, then republican. There had also been the experience of the Commune which, although it was essentially a Parisian manifestation, had led to similar, short-lived manifestations in other cities. There was no certainty that July 1871 was the end of a period of change and uncertainty. All parties and groups showed similar uncertainties. The royalists were split into those who supported the descendant of Charles X (the Comte de Chambord, son of the Duchesse de Berry), who made matters difficult by refusing to accept the three-coloured flag, and those who supported the descendant of Louis-Philippe, the Comte de Paris. The Bonapartists, who were beginning to make their return to the political arena, hardly mentioned the name of Bonaparte (except in Corsica) but pushed the idea of popular sovereignty. The republicans were distrustful of Thiers and sometimes voted radical in order to make sure that the idea of the Republic should be more clearly affirmed. As Thiers was at his most successful, since the country was subscribing to pay for the indemnity and to get rid of the German occupation, he was deserted by the Chambers and forced to resign. He was succeeded by Marshal MacMahon, who was thought to be arranging for the transition to a king. But in 1875, when a former monarchist, Wallon, proposed an amendment which would give the Republic a legal permanency, the Orleanists decided to vote for it. They preferred such a Republic to a more radical version or to a revival of Bonapartism. The

Republic was conservative, therefore it had to be supported. But Wallon's amendment passed by only one vote.

It is customary to emphasize the instability of the Third Republic. It is easy to show this in terms of the difficulty with which Governments were formed and their usual lack of success in staying in power, so that in the years up to 1914 there were more than fifty, with an average life of less than nine months each. This has been given various explanations. The fragmentation and multiplicity of political parties (possibly a reflection of the varied social and ideological state of France) made every Government a coalition Government which could easily break up. There was a decline in Presidential power, particularly after Marshal MacMahon had unsuccessfully tried to impose himself on the Chamber in 1877, and although the constitution gave an important role to the Presidents of the Republic, they tended to become ceremonial figures who did not use their powers (such as dissolving the Chamber of Deputies). There was no corresponding rise in the power of the Prime Minister who remained entirely dependent upon the Chamber and who was therefore forced to play the political game as dictated by the deputies. Thus ministerial instability seemed inseparable from parliamentary government. But there was a deeper form of instability. It often appeared that the regime itself was in danger and that it could easily be transformed into something entirely different. In 1877 when MacMahon attempted to force his views on a staunchly republican Chamber and then dissolved the Chamber (this was the last time a President of the Republic was to do this until 1955), it seemed that there was a possibility of France being dominated by monarchists, aristocrats and army officers. In 1888 and 1889 it seemed as if the Republic might fall under the control of General Boulanger, whose temporary popularity implied a return to strong executive government, but the Government weathered the storm and Boulangism collapsed as rapidly as it had grown. In 1892 the affairs of the Panama Canal Company attracted attention, when it appeared that many officials of the Republic (including deputies) had been bribed into silence concerning the company's bankruptcy. The Dreyfus affair, which began in 1894 with the arrest of a Jewish officer on the charge of selling secrets to the Germans and which became a resounding affair when it appeared that Dreyfus's conviction was unjust, highlighted the differences that existed amongst Frenchmen. In both cases it appeared that the Republic was in the hands of unworthy men and that there were others, often monarchists, Catholics, nationalists, officers, who were ready to take it over. Thus France seemed divided, even decadent.

But behind the political factors there were other elements that showed a much greater stability. There was, for example, the movement of the French population. Whilst the populations of countries such as England and Germany rose rapidly in the years between 1870 and 1914, the French hardly increased in numbers, progressing from 36 million in 1870 to less than 40 million in 1914. In these circumstances it was possible to see the perpetuation of many French conditions and values rather than their transformation. France tended to remain a country with small-scale enterprise, with small towns, small factories, small farms, small commercial establishments. There was neither the vast labour resources, nor the large market for the mass-produced goods that existed everywhere else. Whilst all types of industrial production increased, these increases were in no way comparable to those of countries such as England or Germany, and whilst French inventors and designers were successful in many fields, there was little move to mass-produce their prototypes. In a similar way, whilst French agriculture felt the impact of American, Russian and Australian competition, and incidentally suffered in wine and silk production from the accidents of disease, nevertheless by 1914 about a half of the French population was still engaged in agriculture, and France did not join those countries where agriculture almost perished.

In foreign policy there was also stability. It is true that the acquisition of colonies was not a subject of general agreement, and the formation of the Indo-Chinese Union, the establishment of French protectorates over Tunisia and Morocco, and the acquisition of colonies in West and equatorial Africa and Madagascar led to many disagreements. But once this colonial expansion had been accomplished it was generally seen as an extension of French power and prestige at a time when the defeat by Prussia and the loss of Alsace-Lorraine had reduced her strength and diminished her position. It was Germany, and the considerations attached to German actions, which dominated French foreign policy and caused French diplomats to break out from the isolation into which Bismarck had attempted to confine them. In 1894 the French signed an agreement with Russia which gave France greater security against German aggression, although it increased France's commitments in eastern Europe. In 1904 the Entente Cordiale between France and England put an end to Anglo-French colonial rivalries and, whilst it made no mention of military agreement, it nevertheless paved the way for military and naval discussions and co-operation. Relations improved between France and Italy. So that although there could be many disagreements about the details of French policy, and although the dangers of allying with Russia or the humiliation of giving way to England could be stressed by this or that group, there was a general agreement that France had to face up to the existence and threat of a united, powerful Germany. Even the socialists agreed that the nation should be protected against aggression, however deep their anti-militarism or their conviction that the German workers were their brothers.

Within politics too there was the basis of agreement which could modify division. In order to face up to the Catholic Church's hostility to the Republic and its attachment to the monarchist cause in the 1870s, the republicans had launched an important educational programme. In fact an insistence upon education was to be the main ideology of the Third Republic. In 1879, 1882 and 1886 education was reformed. It was necessary for religious teaching orders to receive authorization from the State; primary education was made free, compulsory and secular for all children aged between six and thirteen; the State imposed its standards upon all teachers in the public educational system. Education and educational methods became uniform; the lingering belief that it was because of their superior educational system that the Prussians had won the war of 1870 caused it to become patriotic in France; the old ideal remained that French unity could be attained through a State system. The number of primary teachers had more than doubled by 1914, more than 85 per cent of children attended school, and they were all taught about the growth of French national unity as they were taught to respect and to appreciate the geographical diversity of their country. Although relations between Church and State fluctuated, and became bad after the Dreyfus affair, with the 1905 law separating Church and State, yet it is possible to see a decline in anti-clericalism. Once it seemed that the State educational system had been fully created, and once it was apparent that there were Catholics who were supporting the Republic, then it was not so necessary to be anti-clerical. The Republic was supported in every village by the schoolmaster. The schoolmaster became a notable and by virtue of his position in society he was the equal of the priest. No one feared any real resuscitation of ecclesiastical rights or tithes. Even such a convinced anti-clerical as Clemenceau who became Prime Minister between 1906 and 1909 declined to enforce all the provisions of the 1905 law which called for the inventory of the Church's property and for its transfer to lay associations. The Republic was prudent.

Another factor that promoted unity was that all the attacks on the Republic seemed to come from the Right. Since the downfall of the Commune it had been the army, the Catholic Church, the monarchists which had attacked, or had threatened to attack, the regime. The result of this was that the Republic began increasingly to appear as something which was worth saving. Perhaps the real significance of the Dreyfus affair was not that it divided Frenchmen but that it brought many together to fight for the cause of justice and truth, and when it was over, whilst there were supporters of Dreyfus, such as Péguy, who suffered from disillusionment, there were many others who were confirmed in their belief that the Republic was something that had to be defended. Those who had been cynical about the Republic and its chances of survival looked back to the affair, and they saw that the Republic had a past and a future. Recalling the affair, at Zola's funeral, Anatole France exclaimed, 'There is only one country in the world where such things could be accomplished. How great is the genius of our country!' A republican ideology emphasized that the Republic was inclusive and that all categories of society were acceptable to it. Even those who believed in future revolution accepted the Republic as the inheritance of anterior revolution.

Prominent amongst those who accepted the Republic, and who had been moved by the Dreyfus affair to proclaim his preoccupation with the welfare of all humanity, was Jean Jaurès. It was only in 1901 that the French socialists had established themselves in two parties, the one led by Jaurès, and in 1905 unity was attained. By 1914 the socialists had a million and a half voters and more than a hundred deputies. But this political movement had little connection with the French trade-union movement. From 1884, when freedom of association was granted (under certain conditions of registration, which were deeply resented and not always followed), and 1895, when the Confédération Générale du Travail brought the unions together, there was a quickening of trade-union activity. But as a movement it was dominated by the doctrines of anarcho-syndicalism, which rejected co-operation with political parties or action within the political system, and looked to direct worker action as the means of replacing the existing state by social and economic arrangements that would create conditions of justice and equality. By 1914 only about 9 per cent of French workers were in trade unions (as compared, say, to 28 per cent in Germany).

In the violent clashes which occurred between workers and their employers, it was always possible for the State to intervene and to crush the workers.

It was true that the social climate deteriorated on the eve of the 1914 war. As with the July Monarchy, there were scandals which suggested that all was not well with the governing élites. The second wife of a prominent statesman and Prime Minister, Joseph Caillaux, shot and killed the editor of the newspaper *Le Figaro* in the spring of 1914. Socialists and trade-unionists insisted that were there a war they would not fight. There were many fears and apprehensions. But the State was strong, with half a million officials employed by it. There was a general prosperity; many classes were experiencing a sense of well-being; there was the comfort of believing that social ascension was to be attained through the republican institution of the school. France was not alone in Europe, as in 1870, and any comparison with that unfortunate year seemed quite irrelevant.

The War 1914–1918

The 1914 war arose out of the affairs of eastern Europe. France was involved in any possible conflict between Russia and Austria-Hungary because Russia was France's ally, and the President of the Republic, Raymond Poincaré, was on a visit to Russia in the crucial month of July 1914, assuring the Russian Government of French support. But France was more immediately involved because of the nature of German war plans. Unwilling to envisage a war against both Russia and France in which two fronts would be active, the Germans had prepared to send an army wheeling through Belgium which would move rapidly and eventually encircle the French army in eastern France. In this way the French would be disposed of militarily and it would be possible for the Germans to concentrate on the more difficult task of defeating the Russians. It did not suit the Germans that France should consider neutrality, since the presence of a French army on Germany's western front would necessitate the keeping of large German forces in the west and would hamper the Russian campaign. In this sense France was condemned to a war and it is interesting to reflect on how little diplomatic opportunity was available to her.

At all events the war was greeted with apparent enthusiasm by many Frenchmen. It was true that socialists and trade-union leaders had been pressing for strike action as a means of preventing their Government, and, they hoped, the Governments of other states, from going to war. Many politicians and observers had protested about the prolonged absence of the President of the Republic, who was accompanied by the Prime Minister, Viviani (they returned on 29 July). But the assassination of Jaurès on 31 July, by an isolated young man who believed that the socialist leader was betraying France, met with universal reprobation. The next day came the news of the German declaration of war on Russia; on 2 August the Germans addressed an ultimatum to Belgium. It seemed clear that Germany was the aggressor. 'They have assassinated Jaurès, we will not assassinate France.' 'The country of the French Revolution is in danger.' 'The France of Voltaire, Diderot, Zola and Jaurès is in danger.' It was with such words that the socialists abandoned all idea of resisting the war. The crowds in the streets shouted 'À Berlin!' and the President of the Republic called for 'l'union sacrée'. The Germans declared war on France on 3 August.

The French army, after a smooth mobilization, numbered some 3,700,000 men. Its commander-in-chief, General Joffre, had presided over the careful elaboration of Plan XVII, which prepared for a French attack in the east, and it was in accordance with this plan that Mulhouse was occupied by forces under General Pau. But immediately things went wrong. The French were forced to withdraw under heavy German fire and it became clear that the German offensive in Belgium was heralding a much more important movement than Joffre had anticipated. By the end of August the French, British and Belgian forces were falling back and the Germans were moving rapidly in the direction of Paris. On 1 September the Government decided to leave Paris and went to Bordeaux; the official communiqués could not conceal the gravity of the situation. But Joffre succeeded in strengthening his forces so as to face the advancing enemy, and when the Germans had shown themselves to be imprudent in their organization, he gave the order to counter-attack on 6 September. After three days of fighting the Germans were in retreat, the immediate danger to Paris was over. What was perhaps more important, the German plan for a quick defeat of France had failed and the Germans were faced with the necessity of fighting a war on two fronts. There was no question but that the allied troops, mainly French, who had been in full retreat for a fortnight, had fought heroically, and that the Battle of the Marne had been a great victory.

Yet the war was not over. The German troops re-established themselves on the Aisne, and before the end of 1914 a continuous front was established from Switzerland to the North Sea. Ten French departments were occupied, including those departments which provided France with most coal, and this occupation, together with destruction and the number of peasants who had been mobilized, meant a substantial drop in French food production. Furthermore, French losses had been very heavy, and by the end of 1914 there were 300,000 French dead, and nearly 600,000 wounded, prisoner or missing. As it became obvious that it was going to be increasingly difficult to relaunch a war of movement, it was clear that such a situation was very unsatisfactory for France. The French army had had to abandon its plans for attacking in the east. France's ally Russia had been heavily defeated (and the French command said, somewhat unjustly, that whilst the French had held five-sixths of the German army, the Russians had allowed themselves to be defeated by the remaining one-sixth). The war, which had generally been thought of as being short, was becoming a long war. In 1915 the French endeavoured to take the offensive in Champagne and in the region of Arras. In February 1916 the Germans started a battle of attrition by attacking Verdun, where General Pétain was placed in command. In July 1916 the British and the French attacked on the Somme. In April 1917 a new general, Nivelle, launched an offensive in Champagne. Not one of these operations had any real effect on the situation; not one of them was successful; every one of them was enormously costly in men's lives.

Since France had traditionally been thought of as a country that was divided, it might have been thought that such a strain as this would have a most disrupting effect. It is true that 'l'union sacrée' was not always effective. The Viviani Government more or less disintegrated in October 1915 and was replaced by one led by Aristide Briand. There were continued disagreements amongst the politicians and the military leaders. French socialists and union-leaders rediscovered their vocations, and in 1915 there were strikes in many of the main industries. By 1917 strikes were much more important and a number of French leaders, such as Caillaux, were flirting with the idea of peace and creating an atmosphere of fear and suspicion. The rumour, in May 1917, that certain French units had mutinied and had refused to take up their positions in the line, seemed destined to cause considerable upset, and a socialist spokesman, Pierre Laval, in a secret session in the Chamber, was quick to denounce the military leaders whose incompetence had led the troops to despair. But in reality French unity persisted, as did the determination to continue the war. The administrative system at the disposal of the Government enabled it to control opinion; the educational system had succeeded in creating a general patriotism. The mutinies were, in fact, both limited and localized, and they had no political content. When the Bolshevik revolution and the Italian defeat at Caporetto seemed to form the climax of a disastrous year, the effect in France was that Clemenceau took power on 16 November 1917. The suggestion that a Clemenceau Government could cause the workers to revolt and result in civil war (since he had brutally broken a whole wave of strikes between 1906 and 1908) was discounted. From that time onwards there was never any doubt that France would fight to the end. Attacking those who were supposedly guilty of treason, Clemenceau created a nervy atmosphere, but it helped him to reinvigorate the nation. Thus when in March 1918 the Germans took the offensive, nearly succeeded in separating the allied armies, once again reached the Marne and were within 75 kilometres of Paris, the French not only held on but on 18 July they counter-attacked. At the beginning of October 1918 the Germans asked the Americans for an armistice. It was eventually signed on 11 November and, since it was a long time before peace negotiations got under way, periodically renewed.

France had lost over 1,300,000 killed (about 16 per cent of those mobilized). For every ten men aged between twenty and forty-five, two had been killed. This was a terrible blow to a country which had experienced a relative decline of population, and even with the recovery of Alsace-Lorraine, the population figures for the 90 departments of 1921 were half a million less than for the 87 departments of 1913. This demographic consequence of the war was of outstanding importance. Compared to it, the wholesale destruction of farms, houses, industries and cattle was a series of minor tragedies. But the financial effects of the war were also devastating. Up to 1914 the franc, which was based on gold, had been one of the most secure currencies in Europe. But the suspension of convertibility, the rise of wartime expenditure, the reluctance to proceed to new taxes, meant that the war had been financed by loans and by an increase in the number of bank-notes in circulation. The consequential rise in prices was considerable, and all those who were dependent upon fixed incomes suffered. France was undoubtedly a poorer country by the end of the war. But in the euphoria of victory such considerations did not seem to matter. With an election expected in 1919 it was only natural that the politicians should join with public opinion in stating that the Germans would pay for everything.

But one thing appeared clear to most Frenchmen. France had won the war, but only at the cost of an enormous sacrifice, and only because, at various moments, France had had as allies England, Russia and the United States. Therefore France had to have security against Germany so that there would be no possible repetition of this catastrophe. From the very start of peace negotiations the French placed the greatest importance in seeking this security. There were those who thought that it would be necessary for Germany to be divided, and that one convenient way of doing this would be by encouraging separatist movements. Then there was the possibility of reducing German strength, both by refusing the Germans the right to have an army and by imposing a crippling economic fine on the German people. There was the suggestion that France should have alliances with Britain and America, and perhaps at the same time with some of the new states of eastern Europe. There were those who thought that if the League of Nations could become an organization with real power, then it could be a means of preserving the peace in Europe and of protecting France. But as the negotiations proceeded the real position of France in Europe became more evident. For economic reasons, there were those countries which did not want to see Germany ruined or divided. Many Frenchmen shared the fear that Germany could become Communist. Neither Great Britain nor America were prepared to commit themselves by treaty to guaranteeing France's frontiers. Other countries saw the League as an eventual means of changing treaty arrangements rather than as a means of maintaining them. The economic difficulties inherent in making Germany pay an indemnity (or reparations) were such that complicated and acrimonious discussions were to continue well into the 1920s and the amount expected was steadily whittled down. The chief French negotiator, Clemenceau, was always conscious of the danger that France would be isolated. France had to be satisfied with an arrangement whereby there was a temporary army of occupation, the Germans agreed to demilitarize the Rhineland area, and France could come to agreements with some of the smaller states of eastern Europe. Such diplomatic achievements hardly seemed fitting after four long years of warfare.

The Inter-War Years 1919–1939

The history of France between the wars is filled with paradox. In the elections of November 1919 a large coalition stretching from the radical to the moderate right wing formed a Bloc National and won nearly three-quarters of the seats, thus preserving the impression of national unity; but within two months a series of intrigues united Catholics and socialists in a successful manœuvre to prevent Clemenceau from becoming President of the Republic in succession to Poincaré. The reconstruction of the devastated areas was carried out swiftly and efficiently, and the 1920s appear as years of considerable progress, with the pre-war production rates easily overtaken by 1925 and with the rapid development of new industries. But these were also years when the Government had great budgetary difficulties, was dependent upon loans, often from quite small investors, and was most insistent upon gaining reparations from Germany. Indeed, more attention was paid to the question of reparations than to the failure of the American Senate to ratify the Treaty of Versailles. It was in December 1920 that the socialist congress at Tours voted for the formation of the Communist party. This party, which attracted an increasing number of supporters during the 1920s, so that in 1928 it received a million votes, declared itself a revolutionary party, believing in the class struggle, affirming its loyalty to Soviet Russia and its opposition to social democracy. But in spite of an important strike movement during 1919 and 1920, the trade-union movement remained weak, was divided into Communists and non-Communists and appeared ineffective. France took part in a considerable number of international conferences in the post-war years, both to discuss reparations and to settle the details of peacemaking. From 1921 onwards it was Aristide Briand who appeared as one of the chief French negotiators, a man whose thought was very European and who started the process of effecting a reconciliation with Germany and a general *détente* in Europe. Yet in 1920 Millerand pursued a policy independent of England over Poland, and sent General Weygand to assist the Poles in their war against the Russians, and more spectacularly Poincaré, who had become Prime Minister in 1922, sent French troops to occupy the Ruhr in January 1923 in order to guarantee the full German payment of reparations. Thus France appeared both as a conciliatory power and as a domineering, nationalist state with the strongest army in Europe.

The sort of difficulty experienced by France is well illustrated by the formation of the Cartel des Gauches and by their electoral victory in May 1924. There was a wide discontent both with and within the Bloc National. There had been a misunderstanding over Poincaré's occupation of the Ruhr. Some had seen in it a deliberate attempt to reduce German power, possibly to dismember united Germany. Those who had followed Poincaré's carefully chosen and legalistic statements were well aware of the fact that his action was to be seen as a means of exacting the terms of the treaty. As the French occupation led to a crisis in the German economy there were those who claimed that even this limited objective was not being attained. The danger of straining both the German political situation and the French financial situation (since the occupation was a costly operation) was pointed out. Internationally the argument was that if Germany was ever to pay reparations, then the allies must first seek to make Germany prosperous. In these circumstances there seemed to be a case for resorting to some new form of foreign policy, and since the movement of an army had not succeeded, then the more idealistic talk of international co-operation was attractive. In addition Poincaré was increasing taxation. In these circumstances the claim of the Cartel des Gauches to represent the republican tradition and to attack the clerical policies of Governments that had sent an ambassador to the Vatican seemed to have a certain resonance.

The premiership of Edouard Herriot was the triumph of the Radical party. This party could look back to Gambetta and could claim to represent the republic in a modern form. Radicals believed in the French State, its centralization and administration, since they believed that what was good for one Frenchman was good for another. They believed that the task of government was to create a better world, and that the principal method of doing this was through an educational system which would emphasize French unity and which would give equality of opportunity. But at the same time the Radicals believed in the individual. Life had to be lived by the individual, he had to make his existence by his own efforts, and not by the intervention of the State. The Radicals believed, with their philosopher who wrote under the name of Alain, that the State should not enrich them, all the more that the State should not impoverish them. They had a vision of a nation of small shopkeepers, peasants and artisans. They saw them as independent, rational, progressive. At times the State was their enemy, when it tried to tax them or inquire into their private lives; but the State was their friend when it came to organize education and to protect them from the aristocracy, the Church, big business, the prejudices of the few or the many. Edouard Herriot appeared as the ideal Frenchman, who had made his way to the Premiership from humble origins because of his scholastic attainments, who was firmly anchored in provincial France through his attachment to Lyon (where he was mayor) and who represented all the aspirations of the ordinary man for peace. It was true that the Left had been united in the elections only, and that the Socialists had refused to share power with the Radicals. This possibly explains a renewal of anti-clericalism which aroused the inevitable riposte of Catholic organizations. It was also true that the Right found itself particularly critical of Herriot's determination to come to agreement with England, since this seemed to imply the abandonment of certain French positions. But the real stumbling block of the Government was the financial crisis. There was disagreement as to how the question of France's finances was to be handled technically, and neither the political leaders nor public opinion seemed to understand the nature of the problem. Essentially the French Government, heavily in debt, was dependent upon public confidence and the willingness of the public to invest in Government bonds. For political reasons, that is to say his need to secure socialist support, Herriot spoke vaguely about taxes on capital, and as the value of the franc declined on the international money market, the possibility of the State being unable to meet its obligations appeared more likely. In these circumstances Herriot was defeated in the Senate and resigned in April 1925, accepting the end of a period of left-wing government by taking office in the succeeding Government which was orientated more to the Right. After considerable confusion and the rapid succession of five Governments in ten months, Poincaré returned to power with a Government that laid claim to be a Government of national unity. This restored confidence, so that capital began to return to France. In June 1928 he stabilized the franc, rendering it convertible but at one-fifth of its pre-war value. From a vague aspiration for reform and progress, France had returned to a traditional leader, who was conservative, moderate and cautious. It was during this same period that Aristide Briand, replacing Herriot at the Quai d'Orsay, established his ascendancy in foreign affairs and claimed to have found security for France in the Locarno agreements, which gave an international guarantee for the French frontiers, and in the Kellogg pact, whereby a number of states renounced force as a method of procedure. When Poincaré retired in July 1929 it could be claimed that up till then, the post-war years had been successful for France. Although it had appeared, during the Herriot Government, that an anti-militarist policy had been temporarily pursued, there had been a general agreement on defence, and plans had been laid for a massive defence construction, the Maginot Line (named after a Minister) in the east. The Battle of Verdun had taught the lesson that a properly fortified defence line could withstand almost any amount of attack. If the French frontiers were protected, then France could be secure.

But succeeding years suggested that France was in no way secure. After a brief post-war increase, the French population continued to decline and it was evident to all that France was a country with an age-ing population. By about 1930 for the first time the urban population of France exceeded the rural population. This disturbed those who believed that a large rural population was necessary for stability, and since France's demographic situation as an industrial state coincided with the great international crisis which began on Wall Street in 1929, this too was inauspicious. Both French industry and agriculture as small, self-financing enterprises, were reasonably well cushioned from the outside world, but from 1931 onwards French trade began to fall back, and the luxury items which formed an important part of the French economy suffered. Unemployment was less serious in France than in other countries but it was all the more dramatic in France because it was less well known. By 1932 production had dropped by a quarter and there were more than 260,000 unemployed. It was parti-cularly tragic that this economic crisis should coincide both with the coming to power of Hitler in Germany (1933) and with the realization of political deadlock at home. The international crisis wiped out all hopes of reparations and one theme of French policy came to a dead end. The resignation of Poincaré removed all idea of consensus, no man and no party succeeded in imposing itself. It was at this time that various groups of extremists began to emerge, sometimes representing those classes in society that were suffering from particular hardship and could identify themselves with a tightly knit organization, such as the ex-servicemen; sometimes representing admiration for the apparently strong Fascist doctrines of other states and expressing common feelings of frustration and apprehension.

In February 1934 the inevitable happened. A scandal surrounding a fairly minor crook called Stavisky suggested that there was corruption in high places, especially amongst the Radicals. A demonstration organ-ized by right-wing groups in Paris led to the deaths of sixteen people and to the resignation of the Government although it still had a parlia-mentary majority. Was 6 February 1934 another French revolution? It seemed not, since the demonstrating groups seemed to have no rational hope of seizing power. But the sense of crisis was so great, the fear of a French Fascism so real, that a remarkable change took place amongst the rank and file of the left-wing organizations. Communists turned to co-operate with the Socialists and Radicals. Possibly they thought that they were making progress and that they could afford to work with bourgeois parties (the number of party members was on the increase); possibly the Soviet Union encouraged this move. At all events a Popular Front emerged and in May 1936 it was this electoral alliance that won the elections. For the first time a left-wing coalition which included the Communists was successful. For the first time too a Government came to power in a movement of popular enthusiasm, with an agreed programme of reforms, and under the leadership of an entirely new man, Léon Blum. The Government of the Popular Front should have marked a turning-point in the history of the Third Republic.

But Léon Blum, whilst remarkably honest and sincere, was also timid and probably lacking in self-confidence. The Communists refused to participate in the actual government, and their presence outside the Ministry was an embarrassment. The electoral victory had been far from complete, the parties of the Popular Front gaining only 55 per cent of the vote and the Radicals being somewhat disgruntled since they actually lost seats. Before the Government could be formed there was an unprecedented wave of strikes which took the unions and political parties entirely by surprise, and whilst this movement probably enabled the Government to push various items of social legislation through (holidays with pay, the forty-hour week, full recognition of collective bargaining), there was the fear in some quarters that violent revolution was just round the corner, whilst in others there was the regret that revolution had been betrayed. Finally there was the outbreak of the Spanish Civil War, which became a subject of tremendous bitterness as the left wing attacked Blum for abandoning his comrades in Spain and the centre urged that France should not get mixed up with things that did not concern her.

By 1937 there was disillusionment with the Popular Front. Blum had devalued the franc, which the Communists regarded as a sell-out and the petit-bourgeois regarded as a tragedy. The cost of living had increased and had absorbed the wage increases of 1936. The movement for reform seemed to have run out of steam. In short, the sense of crisis which had brought the Popular Front together seemed to have passed, in spite of the bad economic and diplomatic situation. From now onwards the Chamber which had elected the Popular Front Government tried to find another Government which was more to the centre. It was these Governments that tried to deal with the international crisis created by Hitler as he extended German power by the absorption of Austria and Czechoslovakia. It was these Governments too that endeavoured to undo some of the work of the Popular Front and encountered in consequence a general strike (in November 1938). The paradox of the inter-war years persisted. The Popular Front Government had created the greatest enthusiasm; but it had also created bitterness, division and disillusionment.

The War 1939–1945

The French Government was linked to Poland in various ways. A convention had been signed in 1921, a treaty in 1925, a military agreement in 1939. The French Committee of National Defence had met on 23 August to decide what it would do if Poland were attacked. It had decided that France had no alternative but to keep her engagements and when on 1 September 1939 German troops crossed the Polish frontier, the French Government ordered a general mobilization. The next day in the Chamber of Deputies the President of the Assembly read a statement condemning the German–Soviet pact which had preceded it. It was noted that the Communists joined in this applause. A message from the President of the Republic recalled Poincaré's call for unity in 1914, a speech by the Prime Minister, Edouard Daladier, recalled that of Viviani at the same time. But the session ended on an ominous note of uncertitude, probably caused by Daladier's belief that a final attempt at some sort of diplomatic settlement of the conflict was in the process of developing. The declaration of war was handed to the German chargé d'affaires on 3 September, but in spite of certain expectations, there was no formation of a Government of *l'union nationale*. The Communist party had had its newspaper seized in August, in September it was dissolved and afterwards a number of Communists, acting in a newly named political group, made suggestions that appeared to be in favour of a negotiated peace. Consequently the immunity of Communist deputies was lifted and a number of Communists (including their leader, Thorez) went into hiding. The Government had difficulty in getting a special powers bill through the Chamber in November and it was widely expected that there would be a number of Cabinet changes. When these did not take place, and when it was suggested that the Government had not done everything in its power to support Finland in its war against Soviet Russia, the majority of the Chamber abstained on a vote of confidence. On 22 March 1940 Paul

Reynaud obtained a vote of confidence for a new Government, in which Daladier remained as Minister for Defence. But if one counts the number of abstentions as well as those who voted against him, his majority was of one vote only (and there was considerable discussion as to whether the counting had been correct). After calling his Ministers together in order to decide whether to continue or not, Reynaud decided to go on.

Thus the war was starting in an atmosphere of confused division for France. Newspapers were always commenting that it was 'just like peacetime'; it was the *drôle de guerre* ('the phoney war'). Apart from a small movement of French troops towards the Saarland, there had been no military action. Five million Frenchmen had been mobilized, but with none of the enthusiasm of 1914. There was no Alsace-Lorraine to recapture, and since there had not been a war over the German occupation of Czechoslovakia it hardly seemed appropriate that there should be a war over Poland. They had spent a cold and inactive winter. Public opinion was either too confident, thinking that the war would be won without a battle and by means of an economic blockade, or too pessimistic, believing that the Germans could never be defeated and that France was engaged in a war which had no hope of military success. French propaganda was put in charge of Jean Giraudoux, the writer and, symbolically perhaps, author of *La Guerre de Troie n'aura pas lieu* (being preferred to another writer Jules Romains, author of *Verdun*); but it had little effect and hardly competed with German propaganda.

It was this atmosphere that many people believe was responsible for the French defeat. It has been suggested that long before the German offensive (which began in Norway and Denmark in April, and attacked Holland, Belgium and Luxemburg on 10 May 1940) the French had no will to fight and no unity in favour of fighting. However, it is hard to explain a military defeat purely in such moral terms. The defeat of the French army requires a military explanation. Nor is it correct to say, as has often been said, that the French army was overwhelmed by superior German equipment. It does seem as if there was a greater parity of force than has often been assumed. It is probably wiser to look at a number of vital factors. Firstly, the French command had prepared for a German move through Holland and Belgium, similar to the Schlieffen Plan. When the Germans attacked the Low Countries they therefore moved their armies to the north (along with the British Expeditionary Force). In fact the main German offensive came through the Ardennes, between Namur and Sedan, and even when the German troops had reached the Meuse, on 12 May, and had started to cross it on the next day, the French command was slow to realize the importance of this. Secondly, there was the fact that the Germans crossed the Meuse, which was a difficult operation, and that they then proceeded to divide the allied armies by moving towards the Channel ports. This meant, as observers such as the British Prime Minister Winston Churchill pointed out during his consultations with the French Government, that the Germans were extending their lines of communication, facing great difficulties of supply and generally speaking they were exposing themselves to counter-attack. Yet the French were never able to mount a successful counter-attack. Whether it was because their commanders were over-trained and over-orthodox, whether it was because they were demoralized by the speed of the German advances and by the impact of weapons such as dive-bombers, the opportunities of taking the offensive were lost. Thirdly, it was in the light of these disasters that Reynaud made a fairly lengthy change in his governmental organization: he replaced the exisiting Commander-in-Chief General Gamelin by the ageing General Weygand who had to be recalled from Syria, the legendary figure of Marshal Pétain became a deputy Prime Minister, and a young officer, General de Gaulle, who had been associated with Reynaud for some time, took a junior post at the War Ministry. Doubtless these changes were inevitable and Reynaud had been anxious to get rid of Gamelin for some time. But precious time was wasted as the new Commander-in-Chief had to familiarize himself with the situation; the fact that he was called in to organize a battle which was already lost caused Weygand to be pessimistic. Thus after the Belgians had capitulated on 27 May, after the British (and some French units) had been evacuated from Dunkirk to England between 27 May and 4 June, when the Germans broke through the defence line which had been organized along the Somme and the Aisne, from Arras to the Maginot Line, then Weygand began to talk of the need to make peace. It was on the 12 June, in one of the châteaux which the fugitive French Government was using as it made its way south, that the question of an armistice was clearly posed for the first time. Two days before this Italy had declared war.

It is inevitable that there should be a great deal of confusion about all these events. A nineteenth-century French writer, Gobineau, has claimed that it is a French characteristic to believe not that they have been defeated but that they have been betrayed. There was much talk of betrayal, and Paul Reynaud had added to this by a broadcast in which he claimed that the bridges over the Meuse which ought to have been blown up had been left intact for the Germans to use (which was, in fact, not true). Equally there were allegations that the French had been let down by the British, especially by British air power. There were fears that a continuation of the war would lead to disturbances amongst the civilian population, even to Communist revolution and to civil war, and these rumours were given a certain credibility by the large number of civilian refugees that were then on the roads fleeing from the German armies and dive-bombers and hampering all forms of military action. Under enormous pressure, and feeling that he could not continue the war if both Weygand and Pétain resigned, as they were threatening to do, Reynaud himself resigned on 16 June. Immediately Marshal Pétain was invited to form a Government which he did very rapidly. He then officially requested an armistice, which was signed on the 25 June.

The speed with which Pétain formed his Government has suggested to some observers that there was a deep-laid plot to end the war and to abolish the Republic. It was certainly true that when the Government and the two Chambers were installed in Bordeaux there was a great deal of intrigue and pressure was brought to bear on many individuals in order that they should accept a Pétain Government. Pierre Laval who had left the Socialists long ago and who had always shown a certain hostility to the war, was prominent amongst them. It is also true that many of those who had always been hostile to the Republic, who had been most cynical about its politicians, and who were Catholics, monarchists, Fascists or various forms of extremist, rallied to the Government of Pétain. The idea was present that everything had gone wrong in France since 1789, and that now was the moment for the 'counter-revolution' to put things right. But none of this adds up to a plot. There was so much confusion in France during 1940 that all one can see is the traditional French approach of personalizing the crisis and confiding the nation to the one elderly (he was eighty-three) soldier whose heroic defence of Verdun in the First World War was the guarantee of his patriotism.

The starting-point of 'Pétainism' was the armistice. By this the Germans occupied about three-fifths of France, the area north of the Loire and the Channel and Atlantic coasts. In the unoccupied zone there was to be a French Government (which eventually settled in Vichy) which would have control of the French colonies, the fleet and a small security force. Thus the first justification was that France had escaped the direct rule which the Germans had inflicted on other defeated territories, such as Poland. To Pétain, as to Pierre Laval, it seemed that with the advantages of this position, they should be able to negotiate and bargain with the Germans on many matters, including the fate of the French prisoners of war and the general economic situation. The better thereby to engage in this negotiation, and with the clear conviction that the war would soon end and that British resistance would collapse, a joint session of those members of the two Chambers voted to empower Pétain to be the Head of State and to promulgate a new constitution.

It is a subject of great controversy whether the Vichy regime was legal or not. General de Gaulle, who had established himself in London on 17 June, and who had on the next day broadcast an appeal to all Frenchmen and women to join him in order to continue the war, maintained that it was illegal, although whilst he was making this claim the British Government was accepting the legality of Vichy. The most telling legal argument against Marshal Pétain is that he did not proceed to any consultation of the French people, a measure which would admittedly have been difficult in the circumstances. But in a sense this argument illustrates the strange position of the Vichy regime. It was a half-way house and it was necessarily a regime that was waiting on events, that is to say, the end of the war. As the war did not end but spread, with the British attacking the French fleet in the summer of 1940 in order to prevent it from falling under German control, with some of the French colonies entering into dissidence with Vichy and eventually with America's entry into the war and the landing of Allied troops in French North Africa in November 1942, the role of Vichy became more uncertain.

It was in any case a very varied regime. It contained its idealists, some of whom believed that a Nazi victory was necessary to preserve the world from Communism, and some of whom believed that it was necessary to organize the renaissance of France by attacking foreign elements within the country (notably the Jews) and by restoring the full powers of the Catholic Church. Then, also idealistic but more technical, were those who believed that there should be a fundamental reorganization of the State, which would be based upon corporations representing occupations and interests rather than democratic principles, and which would bring together and reconcile the forces of capital and labour. This group hoped to see a France which would be dynamic and modern, and for whom the episode of Vichy was the opportunity of getting away from the politicians. They had little in common with their colleagues who emphasized the importance of agriculture and believed in an old, rural France where the traditional values would be revived. Surrounding all these men were the politicians, who simply sought to defend national interests by a continued bargaining with the Germans, and the individual adventurers, in Vichy and in Paris, who profited from the circumstances to further their own interests. At the centre of affairs was Marshal Pétain. His unexpected coming to power had delighted him and with great skill and not a little cunning he endeavoured to steer his way through these difficult waters. Deliberately enigmatic, often silent, sometimes tired and senile, he tried to keep his options open. But as the German chances of victory receded the usefulness of his position declined. His prestige remained and a visit to Paris at the beginning of 1944 confirmed his popularity. But when the Allies landed troops on the coast of Normandy on 6 June 1944 and as the success of the landings grew, then the Vichy regime crumbled. Eventually he was taken to Germany against his will and when he returned to France it was to be arrested and tried for treason.

The Liberation and the Fourth Republic 1944–1958

Whilst the greater part of France was occupied by the Germans (and the Germans had ended the distinction between occupied and unoccupied France with the landings in North Africa) and the Vichy regime was struggling to assert and to define itself, there were two other forms of French government developing, both of which were original in French history. The one was the Government of Free France, subsequently called Fighting France, which General de Gaulle had established in London and, later, in Algiers. This was a movement which cannot be considered apart from the personality of its founder since it was he who largely imposed a unity upon it and whose persistence made it a successful movement. De Gaulle claimed that the Vichy Government did not represent the sovereignty of France because it was dominated by the Germans. He saw his task as being that of saving the national identity of France and of seeing to it that it was not absorbed either by her enemies or by her allies. He claimed to represent France and he promised that when France was liberated, then there would be a great revolution. Justice would be done and the existing French 'establishment', those responsible for the defeats and the betrayal of 1940, would be removed from affairs. This preoccupation with politics and this egocentric approach to the problems of France irritated many people and alarmed others. But de Gaulle's importance was secured by the fact that he succeeded in gaining some sort of control over the other form of activity, which was the Resistance movement on French soil. At first the resistance to the Germans had been a matter for individuals, or at most for fairly small groups. But as time went by the Resistance grew considerably in numbers. The German invasion of Russia in 1941 meant that all Communist organizations turned to Resistance, whereas before this date those Communists in the Resistance had been organized locally rather than nationally. The Vichy persecution of the Jews and of foreigners caused many refugees to become *résistants*, and the decision to send young Frenchmen to work in German factories and the invasion of the unoccupied zone forced many into the movement. It was in 1942 that General de Gaulle's representative Jean Moulin succeeded in creating the National Council of the Resistance before he was tortured to death by the Germans, and although there were very many difficulties between de Gaulle and the National Council, de Gaulle's leadership was accepted.

It was on 6 June 1944 that the Allies invaded Normandy with the intention of establishing a provisional military government until a more regular French administration could be formed. In this they showed their suspicions of de Gaulle and their fear of Communist influence in the Resistance movement. But when on 13 June General de Gaulle was allowed to go to France, and when he went to the town of Bayeux, he was everywhere acclaimed as the leader of France. He appointed his own representatives and before this silent *coup d'état* the Allied military officials melted away. During June and July Allied progress was slow but from 25 July the breakthrough occurred and the process of liberation became rapid. It became all the more rapid because the Resistance movements in all parts of France either hampered the movement of German divisions or themselves successfully liberated whole regions. Typical of these movements was the insurrection of Paris on 19 August which preceded by many hours the arrival of Allied forces (including notably an armoured division of the Fighting French forces under General Leclerc). It was not till 25 August that de Gaulle entered Paris. On 26 August, with the Germans still within striking distance and with enemy snipers still within the city, de Gaulle organized a triumphal parade down the Champs-Élysées to Notre-Dame. It was one of the great moments in the history of France. De Gaulle was universally acclaimed, he was compared to St Louis, it was claimed that the great days of the Revolution were being lived again.

But the liberation of Paris did not mean the end of the war and it was many months before the whole of French territory was freed. The armistice with Germany was signed on 8 May 1945. All this period was a time of violence and bitterness in French life, since not only was there an acute shortage of all the necessities such as food, clothing, fuel and housing, but the Liberation meant the *épuration*, the meting out of justice which both the Gaullists and the Resistance had promised. Those who had collaborated with the Germans were to be punished. This meant that in some areas a sort of reign of terror was established. But although it is difficult to agree on figures and although it is not always easy to distinguish between those who were killed in actual fighting and those who were shot as a punishment for alleged treason, the highest accepted figure is 40,000 and there are those who maintain that it should be as low as 10,000. Both de Gaulle and the Communist party were anxious to avoid any indiscriminate blood-letting. The Communists abandoned any idea of treating the Liberation as the opportunity for a social revolution and the machinery of State was restored. The first Government, formed in September 1944, brought together the personnel of Gaullism, of the Resistance and of certain respectable elements who had been in power before 1940. De Gaulle was thus attempting to group together a large consensus of opinion, and whilst he carried out many of the promises for reform, nationalizing the coal-mines, the Renault motor-works, air-transport, and establishing a social security system, he was clearly anxious that he should appear as the leader of the nation rather than as the leader of any party or group. De Gaulle was also intensely preoccupied with the position of France in the world. He asserted this position in February 1945 by signing a treaty with Soviet Russia and by endeavouring to restore French rule in Indo-China.

It was in October 1945 that having consulted the electorate (including Frenchwomen) by referendum, General de Gaulle received an overwhelming vote to draw up a new constitution. Consequently a Constituent Assembly was elected in which the Communists, Socialists and a new political grouping, the Social Catholics or Movement Républicain Populaire, gained an overwhelming majority. Although its main task was to elaborate the constitution, this Assembly was also able to elect the Government, and although it never voted against General de

Gaulle, he began to find himself ill at ease before it. Possibly he considered that by retiring he would be able to return and impose himself on the Assembly. At all events, after some days of reflection, de Gaulle announced his resignation on 20 January 1946. If he had expected a popular movement in his favour he must have been disappointed. His resignation was accepted with a certain indifference. It marks the end of the period of provisional government.

With the Fourth Republic, as with the Third, it has become customary to stress weakness rather than strength. This was all the more apparent under the Fourth Republic because its birth was difficult and laborious. It was said that before he resigned General de Gaulle was only too conscious of the difficulties of governing since the political parties, which had made no secret of their hostility to him, an outsider who had come on the political scene by dramatically unorthodox means, had rediscovered all their old strength and vivacity. The left-wing majority which dominated the Assembly were agreed on very little and they were not always in touch with the country. Thus the first constitution to be elaborated was rejected by a national referendum. In the new elections which followed the Socialists saw their vote begin to decline and they regarded this as a warning that they should not be too close to the Communists. The second constitution to be drawn up was approved by the country, but with seven million abstentions. Thus there was little enthusiasm for a constitution which reproduced most of the characteristics of the constitution of the Third Republic except limiting still further the powers of the President with regard to dissolving the Chamber of Deputies. The constitution had only one advantage: it existed on paper. But after fresh elections in November 1946, in which the Communists maintained their strong position, it was impossible to find a Government which could command a majority in the Chamber. Therefore, there was a turning towards Léon Blum who accepted to become, in spite of age and fatigue, a temporary Prime Minister until the first President of the Fourth Republic could be elected. Thus it was that when, in January 1947, the former Finance Minister of the Popular Front, Vincent Auriol, was elected President by the two Chambers sitting together, the Fourth Republic resembled nothing so much as the Third.

Yet the crisis of November 1946 was in no way the sort of crisis that the Third Republic had experienced. It was a crisis that was to be typical of the Fourth Republic. At a time of severe economic crisis, with an acute shortage of goods and with a severe inflationary pressure, there seemed to be two sorts of political danger. The one came from the Communists. They had gained an immediate advantage over other left-wing parties because they had shown themselves to be patriotic, particularly after 1941. Their leader Maurice Thorez, when arguing with de Gaulle about the ministerial posts which his party could legitimately claim, had spoken of 75,000 Communists who had died for France. But there is reason to believe that the rise of the Communist party pre-dates the war, and that prior to 1939 there were signs that the Communists were becoming the principal left-wing party. At all events the Communists by 1946 could claim to have either the largest or the second largest party in France (by the elections of 1946 the MRP momentarily outvoted them) and they controlled the largest of the trade unions, the CGT. In this sense there was always a Communist danger. But ever since the Liberation the Communists had collaborated with the Governments. Those Communists (probably few in number) who had thought a Communist revolution possible in 1944 and 1945 had been overruled. There seemed little real danger of a Communist *coup*. On the other hand many, especially the Socialists, were fearful of what de Gaulle would do. Since his resignation he had not retired. In June 1946 he had spoken at Bayeux and had proposed a constitution built around a powerful, active President. At the end of 1946 and the beginning of 1947 the influence of his associates seemed to be considerable, and there were few politicians who were prepared to discount the possibility of a Gaullist *coup*. Finally, in April 1947 de Gaulle founded the rally of the French people (Rassemblement du Peuple Français, or RPF). In May, the Communist Ministers refused their confidence to the Government on the question of wages, and the Socialist Prime Minister, Paul Ramadier, then excluded them from his Government. From this time onwards the two enemies of the Fourth Republic, Communists or Gaullists, were outside the system. The fact that in 1947 and 1948 both these parties were extremely well supported, could only weaken the Republic.

Naturally these movements cannot be explained in terms of what was happening in France alone. The onset of the cold war, typified by the breakdown of the Moscow conference in May 1947, found the French Government essentially on the American side. It was argued that the Russian army was within striking distance of Paris, and it was pointed out that the economic situation in France was such that it was essential to have American aid. But overseas problems were of particular importance. Indo-China had been divided into two, North Vietnam (Viet-Minh) which was independent and Communist, and the south where the emperor Boa Dai was regarded as a French puppet. The outbreak of the Indo-China war, dating from 1947, was to weigh heavily from this time onwards. A rising in Madagascar and nationalist movements in North Africa emphasized the vulnerability of the French colonial system which the Fourth Republic was trying to fit in to a new and more liberal concept of the French Union. At all events, 1947 and 1948 were 'les années terribles'. France had to fit in to the cold war with social conflicts, political instability, economic crisis and colonial difficulties rendering the country weak and, in the eyes of some foreign powers, dispensable.

Yet the Fourth Republic continued. From September 1948 to October 1949 the Prime Minister was Henri Queuille, who had held office under the Third Republic and whose country-doctor approach to matters reduced the tempo of both political and social disputation. In preparation for the elections of 1951, several Governments were concerned with a device (the *loi d'apparentement*) whereby all those parties which were prepared to declare that they were allied together (and this excluded the Communist party) could gain the totality of the seats provided that together they gained 51 per cent of the votes cast. This law was also aimed at the Gaullists who experienced some difficulty in making alliances with centre groups, although there were examples of Gaullists taking part in *apparentements*. The result was that the centre parties gained considerably in seats (if not in votes) with the exception of the MRP. The Communist deputies declined in number and the Gaullists, whilst becoming the largest single party in the Chamber, failed to achieve the massive success that they had expected. The strong position of the centre parties was underlined by the unexpected election of Antoine Pinay as Prime Minister in March 1952. A number of Gaullists broke from their group and voted for him. The next year the Gaullists voted officially for a Prime Minister who was not in their party and they seemed to be less intransigent. In the meantime the Communists, whilst abandoning none of their principles, seemed to becoming a largely ritualistic party.

From June 1954 to February 1955 the Fourth Republic had a particularly dynamic and original Government, headed by Pierre Mendès-France, a member of the Radical party who had been a junior Minister with the Popular Front and who had served with de Gaulle both in Algiers and in the provisional Government from 1944 to 1945. Mendès-France shocked the National Assembly into giving him a majority by promising to end the Indo-Chinese war. This he did by negotiating the Geneva agreements establishing North and South Vietnam as independent states, whilst the French withdrew. He also negotiated an agreement whereby Tunisia became fully independent and no longer a French protectorate. He sought to direct the economy towards greater growth and vitality and he showed a new consciousness of the problems of youth. In European matters France had already taken certain initiatives (the Schuman plan of May 1950, announced by Robert Schuman, then Minister of Foreign Affairs) by putting French and German coal and steel production under joint control. A European Defence Community treaty had also been elaborated which had aroused the opposition both of Communists and Gaullists, whilst splitting the Socialists. Mendès-France undertook a cleaning-up operation and in October 1954 the London agreements allowed for the creation of a German army and for its entry into the North Atlantic Treaty Organization.

It could be argued that the moment was favourable for a Mendèsiste version of the New Deal. The period of reconstruction was largely over by 1951, the deflationist policies followed by Monsieur Pinay in 1952 had held production back, but from 1954 onwards production was increasing and it is possible to speak of an economic growth of about 5 per cent a year. The French economy had been dominated by a regular series of plans, and whilst the first of these plans (1947–53) had been directed essentially towards equipment, the second plan (1954–7) had been more concerned with the consumer. The popularity of Monsieur Mendès-France was associated with the idea that the war in Indo-China had to be ended, that other old quarrels had to be liquidated and that France should be on the move again. Yet this was not to be. A triple opposition was formed against the Prime Minister. The Communists opposed him because he was allowing Germany to rearm, the MRP could not forgive him his failure to support the European Defence Community; and a new subject of alarm grew with the appearance, in November 1954, of an important nationalist revolt in Algeria. It was argued that the man who had made peace in Indo-China might well sign away Algeria. In February 1955 Mendès-France was defeated. His final protest in the Chamber, that the national necessities which he had recognized continued to exist, was seen as an appeal beyond Parliament to the nation, and it aroused great resentment.

Throughout 1955 the divisions amongst the central parties hampered political action. In November the Government was defeated, and the fact that two constitutional crises (that is to say two Governments defeated by an absolute majority) had occurred in a period of less than eighteen months meant that Parliament could be dissolved. A hastily formed Front Républicain of Socialists (led by Guy Mollet), Radicals (led by Mendès-France), ex-Gaullists (led by Chaban-Delmas) and Democratic Republicans (led by François Mitterand) hoped to dominate the elections. But two and a half million voted for a Monsieur Pierre Poujade, almost an unknown, whose party was essentially a party of protest, bringing small farmers, shopkeepers and artisans together through nationalism, anti-parliamentarianism and anti-capitalism. The ex-Gaullists saw their votes slump, whilst the Communists maintained their position (25 per cent of those who voted) and their isolation. Although the Front Républicain formed the Government, Monsieur Mendès-France soon found himself in disaccord with his colleagues and he resigned.

Nevertheless, the Government led by Guy Mollet was the longest of the Fourth Republic. It carried out certain social reforms, such as increasing the length of holidays with pay to three weeks and increasing old age pensions. It began the process of decolonization in Africa south of the Sahara, by laws which gave the direction of domestic affairs to elected African Governments. It bargained hard as the negotiations for a European Economic Community took shape. And it indulged in an adventurous policy when it took part in (and to some extent initiated) the attack on Suez in October–November 1956, an Anglo-French venture, the failure of which caused great resentment in the French armed forces. But, throughout its period in office, Monsieur Mollet's Government was dominated by the Algerian affair. In spite of a considerable military effort and many local successes, the revolution spread. With one million non-Moslems claiming to be French, it had been taken for granted that Algeria was French and was, in fact, a prolongation of metropolitan France. Powerful economic interests, both in France and Algeria, urged that there could be no fundamental change in the nature of the two countries' relations. But it was not merely a question of sentiment or a question of economic pressures. It was precisely a question of power. Given the power of the Europeans in towns such as Algiers, given the power of the armed units in Algeria, and given the existence in Paris of a powerful Algerian lobby, it was never clear that Monsieur Mollet could have any independent policy. His weak political position was worsened by the growth of a budgetary crisis. The high level of consumer demand (which his Government had encouraged) and the high public expenditure, especially on the Algerian war, created difficulties which led to his resignation in May 1957 and the refusal of the Socialists to participate in the formation of another Government.

From then onwards the situation disintegrated. It was clear that the Governments formed had no real solidity. In spite of assurances, the war seemed no nearer to a successful conclusion. Amongst certain of the officers serving in Algeria there grew up the idea that France had become decadent and that the politicians would betray the soldiers. There was, therefore, an atmosphere of conspiracy, made all the more poignant by the suspicion that past Governments had been negotiating secretly with rebel leaders. When Pierre Pflimlin, an MRP leader from Strasbourg, attempted in May 1958 to form the twenty-fourth Government since the de Gaulle Government of November 1945, it appeared to some that Paris was near to abandoning Algeria. On 13 May a Committee of Public Safety, consisting mainly of settlers and students, but effectively controlled by the army, was set up in Algiers.

The crisis that followed was complicated. There were those in Algiers who hoped simply to frighten the Government in Paris. There were those in Paris who sought to impress the rebels in Algiers with their firmness. But there was an undercurrent of implication. The rebellion in Algiers was incomplete. Should it not be extended to metropolitan territory? There were those in the army who thought so and who prepared for such an eventuality. But there were those who were apprehensive of civil war in France and who thought that this would create a Popular Front Government. In these circumstances there was a search for some middle way and there was a turning towards General de Gaulle who had been in virtual retirement since he had allowed the Gaullists in Parliament to vote and act as they wished. That there should have been a turning to de Gaulle was far from being accidental. Without being directly responsible for what had happened, his supporters and agents were deeply involved and were determined that the crisis should end with de Gaulle in power. By and large it would be true to say that many of the instigators of the revolt were only too pleased to get rid of the responsibility for what had happened. And it must be added that de Gaulle showed remarkable political skill as he sought by carefully timed utterances both to reassure and to terrify the political world. But he never lost one thing from sight: that his return to power should be accompanied by a fundamental constitutional revision. Only in this way could he move from the constitution of the Fourth Republic, of which he had always disapproved, to a new and more solid Republic.

The Fifth Republic

There are many ways of approaching the Fifth Republic. The first is through the person of General de Gaulle. It was ironical that de Gaulle, who had restored the Republic with the Liberation, should have been voted into power as the last Prime Minister of the Fourth Republic on 1 June 1958, and should have presided over the creation of the new constitution. The accident of the Algerian crisis gave him the belated opportunity of putting into practice the ideas which he had expressed in 1946, and which essentially consisted of a strong presidential power and a limited role for the Assembly. Thus the Fifth Republic is to be seen as a development which suited de Gaulle and which was a testimony to his skill and to his prestige. After the many frustrations of the Fourth Republic, the patriotism and the devotion of the now elderly (he was sixty-eight) hero of 1940 and 1944 were impressive. But it is also possible to take a more analytical approach. It could be argued that profound changes were taking place in France. As the French population grew and as the economy underwent an increasing number of changes, it seeemed as if the whole structure of French society was on the move. The large number of agricultural workers who were leaving the countryside, the growth of new industries, the spreading of modern means of communication, all meant that France was no longer the country of small towns and small enterprises. The political system which had been based upon this was necessarily doomed. France had to move towards a more modern system and the real irony was that the man who was destined to introduce these changes was essentially a man whose ideology was that of the pre-1914 period. For all that he was haughty, de Gaulle was not a charismatic leader. He was rather an adroit politician, who surrounded himself with competent advisers and who cultivated the art of dramatizing and personalizing affairs. He saw to it that no one forgot the difficult situation of May 1958 when a catastrophic civil war had appeared imminent.

De Gaulle's Government can best be described in several phases, although it must be remembered that he was adept at dealing with different topics at the same time. The first phase concerned institutions.

A new constitution was drawn up and was approved by a considerable majority in a referendum. The point of this constitution was that the powers of Parliament were reduced, and that a President, who appointed a Prime Minister, was the dominant figure in the Government. Elections were held in November and since they were organized on the double-ballot system instead of the proportional representational system which had been used since the Liberation, there were many changes. Although the Communist vote remained steady, Communist representation fell dramatically, and a new Gaullist party, the Union pour la Nouvelle République, gained more votes than anyone. Finally in December a specially designated electoral college, made up of the two Chambers and a number of mayors and municipal councillors, to the number of some 80,000, elected General de Gaulle President of the Republic by an overwhelming majority. The fifth Republic was thus installed, with Michel Debré as Prime Minister.

The next phase was clearly that of Algeria. From the start it had been obvious that the strength of de Gaulle's position in France was the conviction that he and he alone could solve the Algerian problem. Since he had had no direct hand in governmental affairs since the Algerian revolt of 1954, no one had any idea of what his policies were. He deliberately prolonged this uncertainty by the ambiguity of his public speeches, secure in the knowledge of there being no other politician or party in France that was prepared to define a policy. The settlers in Algeria, and some of their supporters in France, including some prominent Gaullists, believed in the complete integration of Algeria with France, and throughout 1959 the idea persisted that de Gaulle would finally come out with this policy. In reality it seems as if de Gaulle was feeling his way, hoping to smash the rebels by a vigorous military campaign and hoping to rally the bulk of the Moslems to him by his personal prestige and a policy of massive investments. By the beginning of 1960, however, some of the extremists in Algiers were convinced that integration was being dropped and they tried to organize another rising, on the model of 13 May. But this time the army remained loyal, and the failure of this revolt strengthened de Gaulle. He was able to reveal that he foresaw the creation of 'une Algérie algérienne'. In April 1961 four generals attempted to seize power in Algiers, in opposition to de Gaulle. It was even rumoured that parachutists would drop on Paris and de Gaulle invoked his emergency powers. But this revolution also petered out. The proof was given that the bulk of the French population did not wish to fight for the maintenance of a French

Algeria, and the Government was able to devote all its energies to negotiations with the rebels (which had already started). Although de Gaulle for a time hoped to preserve French rights in the Sahara, the Evian agreements of March 1962 brought about a cease-fire and implied the complete independence of Algeria. In April a national referendum approved of this policy, 65 per cent of those participating voting in favour. The supporters of French Algeria were reduced to acts of terrorism and the majority of the settlers returned to France.

The third phase of the Fifth Republic began in difficult conditions. General de Gaulle was no longer an indispensable figure since the Algerian war was over. All that persisted was a certain bitterness. Faced with the possibility that the Republic, once its crisis was over, might fall apart, de Gaulle took a number of initiatives. He replaced Michel Debré by Georges Pompidou; in a press conference he deliberately broke with those centre groups who hoped that the European Economic Community would develop into European political unity by insisting on a Europe of independent sovereign states; at the end of the summer, after an unsuccessful attempt had been made to assassinate him, he announced his attention of changing the constitution by referendum. His proposal was that the President of the Republic should be elected by universal suffrage. In response the National Assembly passed a censure motion against the Government. The result was the dissolution of the Assembly, a referendum which approved de Gaulle's proposal, and a general election in November 1962 which increased the majority of the UNR whilst reducing the number of deputies from the centre. The fact that in January 1963 General de Gaulle publicly rejected British entry into the European Economic Community, that in January 1964 he stated that only the President could hold or delegate the authority of the State, that in April 1964 he called attention to France's prosperity, gives the tone to the remainder of this period. National independence, influence in the world, stability and prosperity at home, these were the tenets of triumphant Gaullism. De Gaulle's energy and vision were such that France seemed to dominate Europe and to challenge any idea of an American–Soviet hegemony in world affairs.

But the fourth phase was one of decline. When the first presidential elections, under the new law, were held in December 1965, de Gaulle only gained 43 per cent of the metropolitan votes. In the second ballot he was re-elected with 54·5 per cent of the votes as against his single opponent, François Mitterrand, who had 45·4 per cent. But the fact remained that at the first ballot more than half of the country were against de Gaulle and, even for the second ballot, de Gaulle's majority was far from massive. Then, in spite of careful preparation, the elections of March 1967 were a relative failure for the Gaullists. The UNR retained the majority, but by such a small margin that it was dependent upon the votes of certain deputies representing overseas departments. The Left, both Communist and non-Communist, had made progress, and Pierre Mendès-France, who had always opposed the Fifth Republic and who now appeared as a principal spokesman for the opposition, spoke of the possibility of taking power.

Much of the discontent was explicable. The economic boom had been slowing down; the Government had opted for a stable franc rather than for expansion; there were many sectors of French society which claimed that they were being badly treated. And whilst de Gaulle's foreign policies remained dramatic (in February 1966 he had announced that he would begin to withdraw from NATO since France was an independent nuclear power) there was a certain unease about his activities. His intervention in Canadian affairs ('Vive le Québec libre') and his criticisms of Israel after the Middle East war, were highly controversial.

Yet whilst it was clear that Gaullism was going through a difficult period, the crisis of May 1968 took everyone by surprise. It began with a student revolt, which was nothing very new. The number of students in France had doubled over a period of five years and the protests of this politically conscious group against the inadequacy of university organization had become frequent. But the violence of the pitched battles with the police, particularly in the Latin Quarter on 10 May 1968, was remarkable. Monsieur Pompidou thought it wise to be conciliatory. But within a few days the revolt had spread to industry. Within a week more than nine million people were on strike, the unions had lost control of their members and the political parties did not know what to make of events. Everywhere there was talk of the need for a fundamental change in society.

Whilst Georges Pompidou worked to establish an agreement over wages and working conditions, General de Gaulle seems to have been uncertain as to what to do. His announcement that a referendum would be held concerning profit-sharing and co-management of affairs was hardly taken seriously. Student demonstrations continued, the rank and file of the strikers refused to accept the agreements and it began to appear that the power of the State was disappearing.

Then on 30 May, de Gaulle announced that the Chamber was dissolved and that elections would be held. He claimed, strangely enough, that France was faced with the danger of international Communism. This announcement was all the more dramatic because it had been widely assumed that he would announce his resignation. At all events, the announcement was carefully timed. It coincided with a movement of opinion against the violence and the anarchy which had been so prominent. It provided the opportunity for ending the crisis, and the result was a sweeping UNR victory. This party gained the absolute majority by some fifty-one seats and those (such as Mendès-France) who had been associated with the student revolutionaries were defeated. General de Gaulle chose a new Prime Minister in the person of Monsieur Couve de Murville, and it seemed that yet another phase of Gaullism was about to begin.

But it was not to be. It had been demonstrated only too clearly that Gaullist power could be as fragile as any power. Even within the UNR it was asked whether de Gaulle (now approaching his seventy-eighth birthday) were not a handicap to them. The fact that Georges Pompidou was no longer Prime Minister suggested that an obvious successor was present. An international monetary crisis, the Soviet invasion of Czechoslovakia in August 1968, a feeling of stagnation in European affairs, obliged de Gaulle to look more favourably towards the United States of America and to revise some of his policies. But he insisted upon the administrative reform which he had announced in May 1968. In April 1969 a somewhat clumsily worded referendum was submitted to the electorate. This proposal was for decentralization and for transforming the Senate into a council for the discussion of economic affairs. It aroused the hostility of all the main political parties and little enthusiasm amongst the Gaullists. When it was defeated by a narrow majority General de Gaulle, on 28 April 1969, resigned.

Looking back one is struck by the fact that the proposed reform was defeated by a million votes only, out of nearly thirty million registered voters. But it is also clear that the tendency of policies under the Fifth Republic had been to turn away from personal power. General de Gaulle's popularity, whether measured by referenda, public opinion polls or the presidential election of 1965, had been steadily declining since 1958. On the other hand the so-called Gaullist political party, the UNR, had grown in strength since 1958 and, even allowing for the check of 1967, it had extended its hold throughout the country and was making inroads into regions of France where other political parties traditionally expected support. This original factor in modern French history, together with the customary division of the Left (in 1969 there were Communists, Socialists, Independent Socialists and Trotskyists, all seeking to demonstrate their strength as the true representatives of the Left), explains the comparative ease with which Georges Pompidou was elected President of the Republic, on the second ballot, in June 1969.

It was not easy to succeed to General de Gaulle. Georges Pompidou always said that he would be a President with a style of his own, but that he would adhere to the principles of Gaullism: national independence, the importance of the French role in the world, the unity of the French people. Both Pompidou, who, until 1968 at least, could claim to have been a trusted adviser of the General, and his first Prime Minister, Jacques Chaban-Delmas, asserted that they were in the true tradition of Gaullism. It became almost a customary Presidential riposte to state that he had no need for lessons in Gaullism. But in spite of de Gaulle's discretion and refusal to make any political statements after his resignation, most political observers thought that President Pompidou only showed complete self-assurance after de Gaulle's sudden death in November 1970. This did not prevent the development of certain resentments within the Gaullist group, which were made all the more noticeable because, whilst the President introduced a greater suppleness into the conduct of foreign affairs, and whilst the Prime Minister, proclaiming the need to create a new society, announced a programme of liberal reforms at home, there were indications that the constitutional uncertainties concerning the respective powers of the President and the Prime Minister were helping to create difficulties between the two men. It seemed that the work done in the Prime Minister's office was increasing; at the same time the President's activity was more widespread under Pompidou than it had been under de Gaulle.

Whilst Pompidou showed considerable diplomatic activity throughout the world, especially in the Mediterranean where he tried to establish particular protection for French interests, the principal European problem was that of the European Economic Community. The French Government had shown typical intransigence in the 1970 negotiations to establish economic and monetary co-operation, and had seemed most interested in the common agricultural policy which was beneficial to French farmers; but in May 1971 a meeting between President Pompidou and the British Prime Minister, Edward Heath, provided the Anglo-French agreement which would permit the enlargement of the Community by the admission of Great Britain, Ireland and Denmark (to date officially from 1 January 1973). This change of French policy was explained in various ways. Some saw it as a development which de Gaulle had already envisaged in his closing months of power; some suggested that President Pompidou was anxious to make an Anglo-French understanding the basis of his policy rather than an Anglo-German one, since West Germany, under the Social Democratic Chancellor Brandt, was taking many new initiatives; others preferred to see a French recognition of the permanence of the Community, since the French could no longer threaten to abandon it and, if they were to continue to appear as the dominant power, had to take the initiative in forging new agreements.

At home, after the slow dying down of agitation in the universities and lycées, attention was concentrated on the elections of 1973. They seemed to be particularly significant, since they would be the first elections since the war in which General de Gaulle would not be present as a living influence. Some divisions, and a number of scandals, within Gaullism, and the emergence of a Communist-Socialist-left-wing Radical agreement under the overall leadership of François Mitterrand (Socialist) suggested that the long predominance of Gaullism would be seriously challenged. Foreign policy and domestic affairs were made to come together when the President of the Republic, desirous of using the Gaullist weapon of the referendum, decided to ask the country to approve or disapprove the widening of the European Economic Community. In April 1972 the referendum showed a majority in favour, but the number of absentions (nearly 25 per cent) was a record and the whole operation appeared to be a governmental failure. Consequently and in spite of a recent vote of confidence in the Chamber, President Pompidou replaced Jacques Chaban-Delmas by Pierre Messmer in July 1972. This was a return to a more rigid, and a purer, Gaullism, since Pierre Messmer, who had served for many years as Minister responsible for the army under de Gaulle, had the reputation of being a Gaullist without any liberal tinge. It was a preparation for the elections. It was a reaffirmation of Presidential power (and was followed by a decline in the activities and influence of the Prime Minister's office).

The general election of March 1973 had intrigued and baffled the experts. Communists, Socialists and left-wing Radicals adopted a common programme of sweeping reforms; the Gaullists and their allies ridiculed this programme as impractical and stressed the dangers of Communism; the name of General de Gaulle was hardly mentioned. The result was that the Gaullist majority lost nearly one hundred seats to the left-wing coalition, but, helped by the distribution of electoral boundaries in the country, they retained the majority in the Chamber; the pure Gaullists became more dependent upon the conservative Independent Republican group under its leader, Valéry Giscard d'Estaing, the Minister for Finance; the President of the Republic appointed a non-political personality from his own entourage, Michel Jobert, to be Minister for Foreign Affairs and continued to emphasize the importance of foreign policy and the need to defend French interests before all others. This attitude meant that the French Government had less difficulty than others in adapting itself to the changed circumstances which followed upon the outbreak of the Arab–Israeli war on 8 October 1973. French policy had always been critical of Israel and largely pro-Arab. Changes of French policy within the European Community, such as the floating of the franc in January 1974 and the attempt to make separate agreements to ensure the supply of oil, were regarded as traditional Gaullist attitudes, as was the French insistence on carrying out nuclear tests in the summer of 1973. But dissent amongst Gaullists on a variety of social and political problems preceded the sudden death of President Pompidou in April 1974. The elections which followed were notable for three features. The failure of the Gaullists to be either united or successful; the narrow victory of Giscard d'Estaing at the head of a wide-ranging majority; and the very high poll recorded by the Communist-Socialist and general left-wing coalition under Mitterrand. The new Presidency was said to inaugurate an era of moderate conservatism, concentrating on the immediate problems of inflation and of making the constitution work more effectively. But for many this is still a particular version of a traditional French dilemma, the appearance of the State as both strong and weak.

In other respects there can be no question of the extent of change in France. By the autumn of 1968 the population had passed the 50 million mark and by 1974 it stood at slightly more than 53 millions. Less than thirty per cent of French people now live in rural areas and the number of agricultural workers continues to decrease. With the numbers of teachers, engineers and scientists increasing at a particularly rapid rate, the number of those employed in specialized services must soon exceed the number of those employed in agriculture. But many regions remain uncertain of their future. Deserted agricultural areas and areas of old industry require revitalization; the growth of towns and the increase of the labour force poses problems; the Government's regional policies have still to be seen in practice. There is still a large section of the population which is classified as being poor. There are those who maintain that the first essential is to attack the persistent inequalities of French society. There are those who claim that France is over-bureaucratized and requires a great measure of decentralization. French integration into a European economy and the possibility of a greater association with a European polity still present many different possibilities for the future. And the problem of the unity of the French remains.

Bibliography

Discussion surrounding the French Revolution has always been considerable. Some idea of the controversies concerning its origins and development will be found in the short books by Alice Gérard, La Révolution française: mythes et interprétations 1789–1790 (Paris, 1970) (No. 21 in the series 'Questions d'histoire', Flammarion) and by Jacques Godechot, Les Révolutions 1770–1799 (Paris, 1965) (No. 36 in the series 'Nouvelle Clio', Presses Universitaires). Particularly interesting contributions to the debate are made by Alfred Cobban, The Social Interpretation of the French Revolution (Cambridge, 1964) and Aspects of the French Revolution (London, 1968), who questions some of the assumptions on which many of the most widely accepted accounts of the Revolution have been based, and which are to be found expressed with learning and wisdom in Georges Lefebvre, La Révolution française (Paris, 1963; English translation The French Revolution, 2 vols, London, 1962 and 1964), and Albert Soboul, Précis d'histoire de la Révolution française (Paris, 1962). C. Mazauric, Sur la Révolution française (Paris, 1970), defends a Marxist stand-point. In English the most scrupulous general account is probably to be found in N. Hampson, A Social History of the French Revolution (London, 1963). Two splendidly illustrated volumes by F. Furet and D. Richet, La Révolution française 1965–1966 (English ed. London, 1969), present the Revolution as an amalgam of several revolutions (juridical, urban and peasant) which 'skidded' into a popular and violent revolution, whilst the first three volumes (all of them short) in La Nouvelle Histoire de la France contemporaine, published by the Éditions du Seuil in 1972, cover the whole of the period up to Bonaparte's seizure of power and give full bibliographical references. These are Michel Vovelle, La Chute de la Monarchie 1787–1792; Marc Bouloiseau, La République jacobine 1792–1794; Denis Woronoff, La République bourgeoise, 1794–1799.
    There are a number of studies of particular subjects which are important. The essays by Richard Cobb, The Police and the People (Oxford, 1970), and Reactions to the French Revolution (Oxford, 1972), are always stimulating; the silent world of the peasantry and its links with the Counter-Revolution are analysed by the American sociologist Charles Tilly, The Vendée (London, 1964), and by two

French historians, P. Bois, *Les Paysans de l'ouest* (1960), and M. Faucheux, *L'In-surrection vendéen de 1793* (1964); contacts between revolutionary and counter-revolutionary France and the outside world are described in Jacques Godechot, *La Grande Nation: l'expansion révolutionnaire de la France dans le monde 1789–1799* (Paris, 1956; English translation 1972); one of the great personalities of the revolu-tion, Robespierre, is discussed in a special number of the *Annales historiques de la Révolution Française* (1958). As an example of the way in which local studies are vital for the general understanding of important periods of the Revolution see Colin Lucas, *The Structure of the Terror* (Oxford, 1973), which is a study of the Loiret departement, and J. R. Suratteau, *Le Département de Mont-Terrible sous le régime du Directoire* (Paris, 1964).

Biographies of Napoleon are endless. One which outlines his career with remarkable brevity and clarity is Felix Markham, *Napoleon* (London, 1963), while Vincent Cronin, *Napoleon* (London, 1971), is concerned more with his private life. Many important aspects of Napoleonic France are discussed in a special number of the *Revue d'histoire moderne et contemporaine* (July–September 1970), entitled 'La France à l'époque napoléonienne', whilst G. Lefebvre, *Napoléon* (Paris, 1965), is a survey of both France and Europe during the period. Volumes 4 and 5 of the *Nouvelle Histoire de la France contemporaine* (1972, see above) are short but extremely informative: Louis Bergeron, *L'Épisode napoléonien 1799–1815: aspects intérieurs;* Jacques Lovie and André Palluel, *L'Épisode napoléonien 1799–1815: aspects extérieurs.* They both contain bibliographies.

Traditionally, the downfall of Napoleon and the restoration of the Bourbons was considered by historians as forming a new period in French history which was studied constitutionally in such a work as P. Bastid, *Les Institutions politiques de la monarchie parlementaire 1814–1848* (Paris, 1954), or as economic history in A. L. Dunham, *The Industrial Revolution in France 1815–1848* (New York, 1955). But more recently historians have tended to consider French social history over wider periods. One example is Georges Dupeux, *La Société française 1789–1960* (Paris, 1964), whilst Maurice Agulhon, *La République au village* (Paris, 1970), considers the populations of the Var department from the Revolution to the Second Republic. Two considerable histories, covering a wide time span and delving deeply into social and cultural aspects are by Pierre Sorlin, *La Société française,* Vol. 1, 1840–1914 (Paris, 1969), Vol. 2, 1914–1968 (Paris, 1971), and by Theodore Zeldin, *France 1848–1945,* The Oxford History of Modern Europe (1973). The latter work, which is subtitled 'Ambition, Love and Politics', is the first of two volumes.

The problem of revolutions in France has received a great deal of attention. A theory of revolutions has been put forward by E. Labrousse and has been published in Crouzet, Chaloner and Stern, *Essays in European Economic History 1789–1914* (London, 1970), and one can also consult D. Pinkney, *The French Revolution of 1830* (Princeton, 1972), and G. Duveau, *1848 en France* (Paris, 1948). A remarkable pioneering work on Paris and its population in this period is G. Chevalier, *Classes laborieuses et classes dangereuses à Paris* (Paris, 1958; English translation 1973). Louis Girard, *La IIe République* (Paris, 1968), is a neat account of a short, but rich episode. Individuals are examined in order that a period of history can be the better understood in Douglas Johnson, *Guizot: Aspects of French History 1787–1874* (London, 1963), and F. De Luna, *The French Republic under Cavaignac* (Princeton, 1969). The Second Empire obviously gives good opportunity for the same treatment as shown in J. P. T. Bury, *Napoleon III and the Second Empire* (Paris, 1964), and W. H. C. Smith, *Napoleon III* (1972.) Theodore Zeldin (ed.), *Conflicts in French Society* (London, 1972), consists of a number of excellent essays on various aspects of French life during the Second Empire. The war which ended Napoleon III's rule is the subject of a magnificent work by Michael Howard, *The Franco-Prussian War* (London, 1961).

The Third Republic, from the defeat of 1870 to the defeat of 1940, is outlined in J.-P. Azéma and M. Winock, *La Troisième République* (Paris, 1969), but anyone interested in its beginnings should consult the contributions to the colloquium organized by Jacques Viard, *L'Esprit républicain* (Paris, 1972), and to the colloquium organized for the centenary of the Commune, *La Commune de 1871* (Paris, 1972). S. Edwards, *The Paris Commune 1871* (London, 1971), and J. Rougerie, *Paris libre 1871* (Paris, 1971), are also valuable. The political history of the Third Republic is discussed in F. Goguel, *La Politique des partis sous la Troisième République* (Paris, 1958), is analysed in R. Rémond, *La Droite en France*, 2 vols (Paris, 1968), English translation of 1st ed. (Oxford, 1966), and is vividly narrated in Sir Denis Brogan, *The Development of Modern France* (London, 1967). Certain particular aspects have been studied in detail. The role of Gambetta in the first years of the Third Republic by J. P. T. Bury, *Gambetta and the Making of the Third Republic* (1973) (another volume is to follow); the inescapable *affaire* is discussed in M. Thomas, *L'Affaire sans Dreyfus* (Paris 1961), and in Douglas Johnson, *France and the Dreyfus Affair* (London, 1967); some sidelights of the 1914–18 war are illuminated in J.-J. Becker, *Le Carnet B* (Paris, 1917), and in G. Pedroncini, *Les Mutineries de 1917* (Paris, 1967), whilst the effects of that war and the general economic history of France between the two wars are considered in some detail by A. Sauvy, *Histoire économique de la France entre les deux guerres*, 2 vols (Paris, 1965 and 1967). One of the last great episodes before 1939, the Popular Front, was the subject of a colloquium, *Léon Blum, chef du gouvernement 1936–1937* (Paris, 1967), and is recounted in G. Lefranc, *Histoire du Front Populaire* (Paris, 1965). See too D. R. Watson, *Clemenceau: A Political Biography* (London, 1974).

The war, and the national disaster of 1940, has inevitably created many controversies and an enormous literature. Perhaps A. Horne, *To Lose a Battle: France 1940* (London, 1969), and Henri Michel, *Vichy: Année 40* (Paris, 1966), provide the soundest descriptions of the military defeat and the emergence of the 'État Français'. An American historian has studied the Vichy government, R. O. Paxton, *Vichy France* (New York, 1973), and another American has explored Vichy, the Resistance and Gaullism, P. Novick, *The Resistance versus Vichy* (London, 1968). R. Aron, *Histoire de la Libération*, 2 vols (Paris, 1959), and *Histoire de l'Épuration*, 2 vols (Paris, 1967 and 1969), are not accepted in all their details by some historians, but they remain the most graphic accounts of these remarkable moments in French history. Marcel Baudot, *L'Opinion publique sous l'occupation* (Paris, 1960) (in the series 'Esprit de la Résistance', published by the Presses Universitaires), and Henri Michel, *Les Courants de pensée de la Résistance* (Paris, 1963), are both standard works and likely to remain so, although research is modifying their conclusions.

After the Liberation there came the constitution-making which can be followed in such works as G. Elgey, *La République des illusions* (Paris, 1965),

Dorothy Pickles, *The First Years of the Fourth Republic* (London, 1953), and M. Duverger, *Manuel de droit constitutionnel et de science politique* (Paris, 1948, and many further editions). The relations of France with her colonies and other overseas possessions, which was to be crucial for the Fourth Republic, has been examined with great care for this initial period by an American political scientist, D. Bruce Marshall, *The French Colonial Myth and Constitution-making in the Fourth Republic* (Yale, 1973). The political history of the Fourth and Fifth Republics is neatly outlined, with many references, in J. Chapsal, *La Vie politique en France depuis 1940* (Paris, 1969), whilst good accounts of the Fourth Republic are to be found in J. Fauvet, *La Quatrième République* (Paris, 1959), J. Julliard, *La Quatrième République* (Paris, 1968), Philip Williams, *Politics in Post-War France* (London, 1954). Special aspects of the Fourth Republic have been studied in S. Hoffman and others, *In Search of France* (1963), P. Rouanet, *Mendès-France au pouvoir 1954–1955* (Paris, 1965), Alfred Grosser, *La IVe République et sa politique étrangère* (Paris, 1961), J.-M. Jeanneney, *Forces et faiblesses de l'économie française* (Paris, 1959), and P. Bauchet, *L'Expérience française de planification* (Paris, 1958). Events in Indo-China can be studied in P. Devillers, *Histoire de Vietnam de 1940 à 1952* (Paris, 1952), or in D. Lancaster, *The Emancipation of Indo-China* (1961), but when one tries to get to grips with the war in Algeria, whether in a short pamphlet, such as Raymond Aron, *La Tragédie algérienne* (Paris, 1957), a documentary approach like T. Oppermann, *La Question algérienne* (Paris, 1961), or a broad sociological survey, as is W. B. Quandt, *Revolution and Political leadership 1954–1968* (Cambridge, Mass., 1969), one is inevitably involved in the Fifth Republic. The rising in Algeria, the threat of civil war in France and the problem of de Gaulle's involvement in the various conspiracies that were abroad, have given rise to a great many publications, many of them necessarily polemical or political or both. Perhaps they are best digested in the early pages of a two-volume study by P. Viansson-Ponté, *Histoire de la République gaullienne* (Paris, 1970 and 1971), or in one of the essays in P. Williams, *Wars, Plots and Scandals in Post-War France* (Cambridge, 1970). The subject of the origins of the Fifth Republic is looked at from different angles in R. Girardet, *La Crise militaire française 1945–1962* (Paris, 1964), and in A. Debatty, *Le 13 mai et la presse* (Paris, 1960).

On the constitution of the Fifth Republic there are good accounts in M. Duverger, *La Ve République* (Paris, 1963), and later editions, and in P. Avril, *Le Régime politique de la Cinquième République* (Paris, 1967). Institutions and politics are discussed in C. Debbasch, *L'Administration au pouvoir, fonctionnaires et politiques sous la Ve République* (Paris, 1969), and by two British experts on French government, Dorothy Pickles, *The Government and Politics of France*, 2 vols (London, 1971 and 1973), and J. Hayward, *The One and Indivisible French Republic* (1973). These last carry their discussions well beyond the resignation of de Gaulle in 1969; they contain bibliographies. J. Charlot, *L'U.N.R.: étude du pouvoir au sein d'un parti politique* (Paris, 1967), and *Le Phénomène Gaulliste* (Paris, 1970; English translation 1971), and Annie Kriegel, *Les Communistes français* (Paris, 1968; Chicago ed. 1972), examine the principal opposing parties. For foreign policy there is A. Grosser, *La Politique extérieure de la Ve République* (Paris, 1965; rev. English ed. Toronto, 1967), and Edward L. Morse, *Foreign Policy and Interdependence in Gaullist France* (Princeton, 1973); relevant to the Fifth Republic and Europe, there is J. Newhouse, *De Gaulle and the Anglo-Saxons* (London,

1970), and U. Kitzinger, *Diplomacy and Persuasion* (1973); Wolf Mendl, *Deterrence and Persuasion: French Nuclear Armament in the Context of National Policy 1945–1969*, deals with a fundamental aspect of Gaullist France; on the economy, Andrew Shonfield, *Modern Capitalism* (1965), contains a classical appraisal of what was happening in France, which can be read with the symposium published under the name Atreize, *La Planification française en pratique* (Paris, 1971).

There remains General de Gaulle himself. Out of many, three books can be particularly recommended. Paul-Marie de la Gorce, *De Gaulle entre deux mondes* (Paris, 1964), is a full account but uncritical; Jean Lacouture, *De Gaulle* (1969; English translation 1970), is penetrating; A. Hartley, *Gaullism: the Rise and Fall of a Political Movement* (London, 1972), discusses the General's writings and his actions and provides an acute analysis of both. In addition, Robert Aron, *An Explanation of de Gaulle* (New York, 1966), is short and stimulating. For the events of 1968 there is J. Gretton, *Students and Workers* (London, 1969), which was written close to the crisis, but takes a fairly broad view; for the events of 1969 and what followed, Jean Mauriac, *Mort du Général de Gaulle* (Paris, 1972).

On de Gaulle's successor there is a biography, P. Rouanet, *Pompidou* (Paris, 1969). On President Pompidou's first Prime Minister, Jacques Chaban-Delmas, it was his downfall which attracted the attention of P. Alexandre, *Exécution d'un homme politique* (Paris, 1973). The major political event of the first four years of M. Pompidou's Presidency, the general election of 1973, can be studied in Un Dossier du Monde, *Les Forces politiques et les élections de mars 1973* (Paris, 1973). See too Charles Debbasch, *La France de Pompidou* (Paris, 1974).

For a general assessment of the state of France there are three thought-provoking books: Michel Crozier, *La Société bloquée* (Paris, 1970); John Ardagh, *The New France* (1970); Pierre George, *France* (1967; English translation 1973). For recent events *L'Année politique* and the *Revue française de science politique* are regular publications which should be consulted.

INDEX